King of Eagles

The Most Remarkable Coin Ever Produced by the U.S. Mint

DEAN ALBANESE

HARRIS MEDIA

Packaged and copublished by Harris Media and Publishers Solutions, LLC. Discounts on bulk quantities of this book are available to corporations, professional associations, and other organizations. For more information visit www.KingofEaglesCoin.com.

Manufactured in the United States of America.

Library of Congress Control Number: 2009928657

FIRST EDITION
10 9 8 7 6 5 4 3 2 1

ISBN-13: 978-0-9799475-2-0

Acknowledgments

We wish to extend our thanks and appreciation to the following companies for their help and support and the wonderful color images in this book.

Collectors Universe, P. O. Box 6280, Newport Beach, CA 92658
<www.collectors.com>

Heritage Auction Galleries, 3500 Maple Avenue, Dallas, TX 75219
<www.HA.com>

Stack's, 123 West 57th Street, New York, NY 10019 <www.stacks.com>. Photographs courtesy of Stack's, which includes illustrations from *Stack's and American Numismatic Rarities.*

CONTENTS

Acknowledgments

My deepest thanks and appreciation go first to God, for making all things possible.

I would like to thank John Albanese, a friend, mentor and a gentleman with impeccable integrity in the field of numismatics. Thank you to my wonderful staff at Albanese Rare Coins, Bonnie Sabel, Dominic Albanese, Darrin Albanese, my father, David the Coin Ace, Robyn Moore, and Richard Rosario for their advice and support; to those who contributed their knowledge, advice, and enthusiasm, Ed Reiter, Joe Rosson, Robert W. Julian, Dorothy Harris, Eric P. Newman, David Alexander, Tom DeLorey, Scott Travers, Joe Galli, Bob Higgins, Don Ketterling, Charlie Brown, Dave Borner, Mark Feld, David Bowers, Kris Karstedt, Melissa Karstedt, Andrew Bowers, and Brenda Bishop; to all of the American Numismatic Association (ANA) staff members who helped me at the museum and library, where I joyfully sat for countless hours researching and writing; and to Mark Feld, Kenny Duncan, Katie Duncan, and Laura and George at Legend.

A special note of appreciation goes to all of our wonderful clients who keep our business going and keep believing in us!

Last, but certainly not least, I offer my thanks and love to my parents and, most of all, to my three children, Dominic, Marella, and David.

— *Dean Albanese*

FOREWORD

The Rodgers and Hammerstein musical *The King and I* features a lovely song called "We Kiss in a Shadow," set in the Kingdom of Siam in the nineteenth century. In it, one of the king's concubines and her secret lover lament that they must meet surreptitiously, lest they be discovered and punished.

What does this have to do with the 1804 Plain-4 Proof Eagle? Symbolically, quite a bit. Like the star-crossed lovers, this majestic gold coin has been unjustly consigned to the shadows — and, like them, the coin is closely linked to the 1800s Siamese monarchy.

Siam was one of the stops where a U.S. envoy, sent to establish trade relations, left behind a Proof set of this nation's current coins as a token of friendship from President Andrew Jackson. Indeed, the "King of Siam set" was the key to unlocking the puzzle of the 1804 Dollar, whose origins had been clouded in mystery for more than a century.

It is not often mentioned, but the same solution also helped explain the origins of the Dollar's golden companion, the Plain-4 Eagle.

Most longtime coin collectors know the story of how the U.S. Mint came to produce silver Dollars dated 1804 for inclusion in these sets — even though all of the coins were struck three decades later. The 1804 silver Dollar has long been acclaimed "The King of American Coins," and the fifteen known examples routinely bring record prices whenever they come up for sale.

Confounding, however, is that far fewer hobbyists have paid similar attention, and similar homage, to the 1804 Plain-4 Proof Eagle, even though both coins share the same historical roots and were part of the same romantic journey to far-off lands, and even though the Eagle is nearly four times rarer than the Dollar.

In this book, Dean Albanese takes a long-overdue look at this old familiar story from a fresh new perspective — that of the Eagle, not the Dollar. Eric P. Newman and Kenneth E. Bressett answered the question of how both coins came about in their landmark 1962 book *The Fantastic 1804 Dollar*. But that was aimed primarily at providing a plausible theory for the minting of the Dollar — which, after all, has captured the hobby's collective imagination for generations. Consequently, its focus was on the Dollar.

Now, *King of Eagles* shifts the spotlight and makes a persuasive case that the Eagle richly deserves hobbyists' adulation in its own right.

Albanese has been making that case in his personal dealings for years and has validated this view by selling one of the four known examples of the Plain-4 Proof Eagle not once, not twice, but three times, for seven-figure sums — most recently, in 2008, for a staggering $5 million. As of this writing, that is almost $1 million more than the highest recorded price for any 1804 silver Dollar.

In nearly forty years as a writer, an editor, and a columnist for leading numismatic periodicals, I have witnessed the public sale of multiple examples of the 1804 silver Dollar. However, I have covered just one auction involving an 1804 Plain-4 Proof Eagle — that of Louis Eliasberg's U.S. gold coins in 1982. That has been the only auction appearance of a Plain-4 Proof Eagle since 1955.

Typically, the coin got nowhere near the respect it should have had, even though the gallery included many of the most knowledgeable numismatic experts in the country. It fetched just $33,000 — less than 5 percent of the sale's top price of $687,500.

Overlooked and overshadowed — that was the story of this magnificent Eagle's life until Albanese decided to rewrite it, with support and encouragement from his father, David Albanese, the other principal in their family coin business.

Now this King of Eagles is soaring to the heights it should have reached decades ago. And thanks to this highly readable, thoroughly engrossing book, it will never be consigned to live in the shadows again.

Its place in the sun will be secure.

— *Ed Reiter*

King of Eagles

The Most Remarkable Coin Ever Produced by the U.S. Mint

INTRODUCTION

Tales about gold abound, from the legendary King Midas to the $2 billion in Nazi gold that vanished in the chaos of 1945. I, too, have a tale to tell — the story of one of the most beautiful, fascinating, and undervalued coins ever minted by Uncle Sam.

The subject of my story is the 1804 Plain-4 Proof Eagle, or $10 gold piece. As pointed out by specialists in early nineteenth-century numismatics, the 1804 Plain-4 Proof Eagle has long been overshadowed by the much more famous 1804 silver Dollar, a rarity acclaimed by generations of collectors as the "King of American Coins."

Perhaps before we go on, I should explain what I mean by the "1804 Plain-4 Proof Eagle," because I am sure many of you are wondering whether there are other types of 1804 $10 gold coins than the one primarily discussed here. The answer is yes — the "1804 Crosslet-4 Eagle," of which 3,757 were made in 1804 (approximately 2 percent of these are thought to have survived the melting pot). And then there is the "1804 Plain-4 Proof Eagle," of which only four were made — two in December 1834 and two in April 1835, for diplomatic purposes.

"Proof" means that these 1804-dated coins were made with dies that had been polished for the purpose of minting special specimens that had a mirrorlike finish. Most Proof coins are struck twice so the designs are fully brought up and, therefore, have a sharp image with great detail.

This eclipsing of the 1804 Plain-4 Proof Eagle by the 1804 silver Dollar is a situation that has been reflected through the years, not only in the vastly greater publicity enjoyed by the silver Dollar but also in the substantially higher prices it has historically realized. Yet both coins share common origins, having been struck not in 1804 but in 1834 and 1835 for special presentation sets to foreign governments such as Siam and the sultanate of Muscat (modern-day Oman). Some silver Dollars dated 1804 were restruck from original dies in the late 1850s at the U.S. Mint, but these were not authorized.

Both coins, therefore, share — or should share — the mystique, charisma, and magic that derive from the unusual history of these sets. The Plain-4 Proof Eagle is much rarer than the 1804 silver Dollar, because whereas there are only four known Proof Eagles with that date, there are fifteen specimens of the 1804 silver Dollar (including seven restrikes) currently acknowledged by collectors.

It is understandable why others may have shied away from writing about this coin, because it has a murky history, and it is almost impossible to come up with complete pedigrees for the four known specimens. With the 1804 silver Dollars, numismatic researchers have compiled detailed histories of all the known examples, documenting who owned each specimen down through the decades, and when and how each change of possession occurred.

Sadly, no similar records have ever been pieced together for the Plain-4 Proof Eagle. To be sure, the royal presentation set made for the king of Siam is still largely intact (two silver coins are missing) in its original case, but what of the Eagles in the sets reportedly sent to Muscat (Oman), Japan, and Cochin China (Vietnam)? I will discuss this fully a bit later and offer my opinion of where these coins are now and where they have been over the past 175 or so years.

Countless hours have been spent tracking down, studying, and analyzing the fragments of information available from various sources about the provenances of these four coins. I have been fortunate enough to have viewed (and to have marveled over) all four of these extremely rare disks of gold. I have pondered the paths they have traveled and noted the subtle differences that set each coin apart from the others.

In my relatively brief career as a coin dealer, I have had the privilege of finding a new home for one of these exquisite coins on three different occasions. Few people in the trade have been so fortunate, but one of them was Thomas L. Elder, a prominent New York City dealer who handled Plain-4 Proof Eagles in two separate auction sales — one in 1911 and the other in 1935.

Rather inexplicably, Elder did not remember the 1911 sale when he described the coin for sale in the 1935 E. H. Adams and F. Y. Parker Collection catalog as:

> **1804 Gold. The regular issue. Figure 4 just touches the bust. Reverse: Heraldic eagle. First three stars at left touch clouds. Edge milled. Brilliant Proof. Excessively rare. Only 4 struck! Cost $500, and rarer than an 1804 dollar. First seen by us.**

Evidently, the fabulously rare coin had not made much of an impression on Elder almost a quarter of a century earlier. It is mind-boggling to think that he did not even remember having handled it before! That, as much as anything, sums up the status of this much-overlooked coin — then and now — as an underappreciated, first-magnitude star in the galaxy of American numismatics. Its value has risen dramatically since the 1930s, but it is still greatly underpriced relative to other major rarities.

I, for one, not only appreciate the Plain-4 Proof 1804 Eagle, I am completely enthralled. It has become my personal crusade to share this passion with others by giving this magnificent coin the kind of glittering showcase it so richly deserves. Join me, then, on this journey of discovery as I lovingly explore the largely uncharted world of this "superstar in the shadows" — the glorious Plain-4 Proof 1804 Eagle that has yet to have its day in the sun.

LIBERTY

CHAPTER ONE

THE EAGLE AND I

It was a cold, snowy day in Rochester, New York. I was sitting in the private airport lounge glaring at the wintry scene through the big foggy windows after my head of security — who happens to be my brother Dominic — dropped me off to wait for my flight to California. The wind was blowing, and I thought I could feel the frigid breath of Lake Ontario cutting through the glass and then ricocheting around the building.

I remember the time — it was 2:10 p.m., February 10, 2005 — and I was waiting for my new client to pick me up in his private Falcon 900 jet. I had never experienced the feelings that were spinning around in my head and churning in the pit of my stomach. I was so excited to have a relationship with a new client who was about to change my life forever. This individual had a fervor for true rarities and, more importantly, perhaps, the money to passionately pursue and obtain what I would call "museum-quality coins."

Some people might carry loose change in their pockets, but I was carrying — secreted here and there — some prime gold Eagle rarities (an "Eagle" is a U.S. gold coin with a $10 denomination). These included an 1867 Liberty Head $10 in PR64DCAM (Proof-64 Deep Cameo) condition, a coin with a mintage of fifty coins, with only about a dozen surviving to this day; an 1880 Liberty $10 in PF66 Ultra Cameo, a coin with a mintage of only thirty-six coins; and an 1881 Liberty $10, also in PF66 Ultra Cameo with a mintage of only forty coins and a survivorship of about ten pieces.

In addition, I was tightly holding on to (yes, I was more than a little nervous) an 1882 Liberty Head Eagle graded PR65CAM, a coin with a mintage of only forty coins and a total survival of about thirteen specimens. On top of this, I was concealing some other extremely rare Proof Double Eagles ($20 U.S. gold coins) in high grades. But this meeting was about Eagles, and this man wanted the best that money could buy.

I was in the airport that day because my new client, James, had been watching my Web page. He was doing extensive research on coin dealers around the country and was checking out many of the major players in the field, and for some reason he decided to call our office. Thank heaven my father answered the phone, because he is one of the nicest people who has ever walked the earth and a real "people" person — to use something of a cliché.

James told my father that he was interested in rare coins and actually wanted to fly in from California with his wife to meet us and to look over some interesting coins and maybe pick out a few for his collection. In anticipation of the visit, we gathered some special specimens from Bob Higgins, a wholesaler who happened to be my mentor in the coin business and family friend. The next day, James and his wife suddenly appeared in our office.

I was sitting at my desk and scanning some coins for our Web page. At the edge of my peripheral vision I saw a man and woman dressed in jeans and sweaters who appeared to be just "regular people." I was impressed when the woman noticed hanging on the wall all of the autographs that I had collected over the years. The man, who turned out to be James, noticed a movie poster promoting *The Godfather, Part 1* — the one that featured Michael Corleone sitting in his father's chair with Don Vito Corleone standing beside him with his hand on Michael's

Putting Our Coins on the Table

This is a short list of some of the coins that were on the card table and why these particular coins are considered valuable:

1. **The 1915-S Panama-Pacific Exposition $50 gold commemorative, round shape in MS67 (Mint State-67) condition (Octagonal $50 gold pieces also were made, but the round ones are rarer).** Originally 1,500 of these rather large coins were minted at the San Francisco Mint, but only 483 were sold — the rest were melted down. This coin and one other coin are considered the absolute finest of these $50 round Panama-Pacific rounds, and they have been called the "Best of the Best" by the Numismatic Guaranty Corporation, a coin grading service widely known as NGC.
2. **The 1861 gold Double Eagle ($20) in PF67 Ultra Cameo.** While 2,976,453 of these coins were minted, only sixty-six were minted as Proof coins. Today, there are only six surviving coins. One is in the Smithsonian Institution and another is in the American Numismatic Society collection, but this PF67 Ultra Cameo is the finest-known specimen available for sale.
3. **The 1881 gold Double Eagle ($20) in PF66 Ultra Cameo condition.** There were only 2,260 of these coins minted, and only sixty-one were Proofs. There are only ten to twelve surviving coins, and this one is the single-finest specimen known for this date.
4. **The 1876 gold Eagle ($10) in PR65 condition.** The mintage for this year was just 732 coins, and only twenty coins were made as Proofs. It is thought that only eight to ten survive, and this is the single-finest example known.
5. **The 1829 "Capped Head Large Date" gold Half Eagle ($5) in MS66 condition.** This coin is from the famous Bass collection and once belonged to King Farouk of Egypt. The total surviving population of Half Eagles with this large 1829 date is thought to be just four coins, and this has been described as a "true coin for the ages."
6. **The 1879 gold "Stella" ($4), coiled hair, in PF67 condition.** Only ten of these coins were minted, and this one is tied with another for the finest-known specimen.
7. **The 1875 $3 gold piece, "Indian Princess," in PF64 condition.** This coin was minted only in Proofs, and only twenty were struck. This coin is considered "one of the most famous rarities in American coinage."

1915-S Pan-Pacific $50 Round (Photo courtesy of Stack's)

shoulder and said, "Look honey, he has a poster with the Corleones — I love *The Godfather* — this is great."

This broke the ice, and James's warm, genuine smile and firm handshake told me that he was a real down-to-earth person with no image he felt he had to project. I shut down my computer and the three of us walked over to an ordinary card table that had been set up. There were two chairs and a couch for viewing and about $5 million of rare coins spread out rather haphazardly on the top. James's first comment was, "Well, this is interesting, to say the least." We all laughed, but in my head I was hoping that he was not judging us by our disorganization.

Over the card table, James looked at me and said, "I'll tell you the truth, I don't know where to begin. I know I want to start collecting coins as a hobby, but I don't have any direction." At this point, I had no idea what he was really interested in and no idea of how much money he was capable of spending. I knew from the phone conversation that he wanted to buy rarities, but I still had no clue whether grades were more important to him or if rarity and denomination were more central to his desire to collect.

I decided to be blunt and asked him, "What price range are you looking to spend, and what type of coins turn you on the most?" James shot back, "Turn me on?" as if he had no idea what I was talking about. "Yeah," I replied, "When you look down at all these coins, I want to know what intrigues you the most, what catches your eye first." This was an interesting query, because we had coins on the table that ranged in value from $1,000 to $1 million, but he did not know which ones had the highest price tags and which ones had the lowest.

As a sort of test, my father handed him a $3 gold piece (these coins were minted for a relatively short time between 1854 and 1889). It was a business strike with a high MS grade. Let me clarify — a "business strike" is a coin that was minted to be circulated as money rather than minted for collectors and not intended for circulation. "MS" means "mint state," and is a term applied to uncirculated coins in a range from MS60 to MS70. An "MS70" coin is one that is absolutely perfect with no blemishes, a flawless strike, and has good color, along with other characteristics that meet the highest standards.

James held the coin up and asked, "Do you like this? Because if you really think it is rare and nice, I will buy it." This is a risky statement for a coin collector to make to a coin dealer whom he does not know really well, but I remembered what it was like when I first came into the coin industry and was taken advantage of by dealers who had more knowledge than I did.

So I picked up the coin, examined it for perhaps three seconds, and said, "No, to be honest, I really do not like it." Now James got a really baffled look on his face, and he must have been thinking, "If this coin is not all that wonderful, then why is it out here for sale?" "Why don't you like it, Dean?" he finally inquired, and I explained to him that I did not like it because — in my professional opinion — it had not been graded properly.

The coin appeared to have been rated too high and was, therefore, more expensive than it should have been and probably not a good investment. It was priced in the high five figures, and I thought that it was not something that I could recommend. James then asked the proverbial $64,000 question, or perhaps in this case it was the multi-million-dollar question: "For my collecting, what should I be searching for to buy?"

I answered him straight from my heart. I told him that I thought he should be purchasing and investing in $10 gold pieces or Eagles. I went on to explain that I felt exceptional examples of Eagles could be found — if a collector has a substantial amount of money. Eagles are not impossible to find, and it was my opinion that rare Proof gold Eagles were somewhat undervalued. This is especially true when the prices realized for the 1804 Proof silver Dollar are compared to the price paid for the 1804 Plain-4 Proof Eagle that I had sold two years earlier. This really got James's attention, and he looked at me with amazement and said, "You handled the 1804 Plain-4 Proof Eagle!?"

My father and I had found in 2003 the finest-known, most gorgeous example (at least to my eyes) of the 1804 Plain-4 Proof Eagle in PF64 Cameo as certified by the Numismatic Guaranty Corporation (NGC). The word "Cameo" refers to the depth of the mirror finish on a Proof coin — other words used are "Deep Cameo" and "Ultra Cameo." The number 64 refers to the condition of the coin on a scale of 1 to 70.

At this point, the history of the coin that my father and I found gets a little controversial, because the example we handled was rumored to be the original Eagle from the set presented to the king of Siam by the U.S. government on April 6, 1836. This is a well-known set that has an 1804 Plain-4 Eagle in it that some feel may be a replacement, because its condition is not quite up to par. The coin we had was exceptionally beautiful, and some think it was the original coin in the King of Siam set, but more on that later.

I told James that we had indeed handled the 1804 Plain-4 Eagle and asked if it was something in which he might be interested. He answered with an emphatic "Yes!" Now I knew how serious my new client was — he was willing to diligently pursue the Holy Grail just like the Arthurian knights of old. Or, like Jason of Argonaut fame, he was ready and willing to seek the Golden Fleece, and in the same manner as the Spanish Conquistadors, he was looking for the fabled "El Dorado"!

My father and I had sold the 1804 Plain-4 Eagle to a foreign businessman who admired it for its great beauty and appreciated it for its rarity. He also understood — just as we did — that his coin was greatly undervalued when you consider that the 1804 silver Dollar had sold in 1999 for $4,140,000, and that there were fifteen of these known to exist. But only four 1804 Plain-4 Proof Eagles are known to exist, which makes this a much rarer coin, and one that should fetch a considerably higher price.

As I just said, only four of these coins are known to exist. One is on long-term loan by the Harry W. Bass Jr. Foundation in the American Numismatic Association Money Museum in Colorado Springs, the second is in the King of Siam grouping, the third is in a private collection, and the fourth is the one sold by my father and me.

James's interest in the 1804 Plain-4 Eagle presented the possibility of bringing this coin back to the United States so that all four specimens could once again be on American soil. This was very exciting to me. With James's interest established, I smiled and told him that the only way he could hope to own this historic treasure was to be prepared to spend approximately $2 million. I knew this because the client to whom we had originally sold the coin said he loved it so much that he would not consider parting with it for less.

James just looked at me and said, "Let's just finish this first deal, and then we can talk about that." That night, James and his wife bought more than $500,000 worth of rare coins — beauties that could take your breath away and have you staring at them for hours without knowing

Adam Eckfeldt

how much time had actually passed. In short, they were mesmerizing.

The next morning, my brother Dominic took James and his wife back to the airport, and James called me to say that he would be in touch because he wanted to send his plane back to fly me to Southern California to talk about the "Holy Grail" — the 1804 Plain-4 Eagle.

Now here I am in the ice-cold Rochester airport and James's plane has just landed. I am anxious, to say the very least. I have never sold anything this big before, and I have never dealt with a client of this caliber and at this level. I was excited!

On the plane, James and I discussed great collectors in my area, and we chatted about how amazing, how underappreciated, and how undervalued the 1804 Plain-4 Eagle was. After landing in Southern California, we went to James's home and talked for the next seventeen hours, without stopping for sleep. We talked about why he had chosen my company (and me) to represent him. He said he had researched forty different firms and individuals before choosing us.

James has a great interest in history, and on top of that, he is a collector. I was impressed, for example, that he has Napoleon Bonaparte's sword hanging on the wall in his home. We talked about coin history, particularly the romance of the 1804 silver Dollar and Plain-4 gold Eagle.

At the end of our talk, James said that he wanted to be an investor. He went on to say that he looked at the 1804 Plain-4 Eagle as an important numismatic part of history and "home run" that only he could make. We also decided that we wanted to make the world more aware of this fabulous coin that was so unfairly eclipsed by its much more common cousin, the 1804 silver Dollar, and we decided that I would write this book after the adventure was over.

The decision to purchase the coin for $2 million was rather quickly made, and I went home to contact the collector to whom I had sold the 1804 Plain-4 gold coin just a few years earlier. I had originally sold it to him for $900,000 and had promised him at the time that if he ever wanted to sell it again, I could get him a $1 million profit.

The negotiations were surprisingly difficult, and at one point the seller actually reneged on the deal. It took weeks and weeks of conversations, and I had many a sleepless night until an agreement was finally reached. The big hang-up was that James wanted to buy the coin over a year's time, but the seller needed money right away. In the end, we managed to concur on all of the details, and the seller was very happy because he was making $1.1 million after only a year and a half on a $900,000 investment.

The only worrisome detail was that I had to go and pick up the coin personally in Baltimore, Maryland. In addition, the seller had sold James an 1838 Eagle in Proof 65 condition (only two are known in this state) for $1.2 million, and I had to bring that coin back as well.

The 1838 Proof Eagle is a remarkable coin that was minted for collectors only. The U.S. Mint's chief coiner, Adam Eckfeldt, had made Proof coins available on a semiregular basis beginning in 1817, and by the 1830s Eckfeldt was making these special coins in most denominations struck at the U.S. Mint. This continued until Eckfeldt retired in 1839, but his successor, Franklin Peale, continued the practice during the 1840s.

I drove to Baltimore with my brother Dominic for security, and as we got closer, my anxiety grew, but we met the seller in a hotel and safely collected the two coins. I casually put the $3.2 million coins in my pocket and reversed my route back up the Eastern seaboard, across New York State to home.

To use a rather hackneyed but accurate phrase, I was sweating bullets as we drove across the country. I envisioned hijackings, fiery crashes, crazed lunatics, and kamikaze drivers. I must have checked my pocket 100 times on the way home just to make sure the incredibly rare coins were still there.

I felt a little like James Bond on a secret mission, but fortunately nothing exciting happened. (Was I a bit disappointed? Well, maybe just a little.) We arrived home with no difficulty, and I immediately called James. All I had to say was "The Eagle has landed!"

Once again James's plane arrived at Rochester airport to take the treasure I had just acquired and me back to Southern California. Once I was there, I just laid the two coins out on a table. I felt like it was the most wonderful magic trick; hocus-pocus — the treasure of Xanadu!

But James's wife had some reservations. She had just seen her husband spend $3.2 million on two rather small pieces of gold, and all they had was my assurance that when it came time to sell them, they would have a tidy return on their investment. I had promised at least a $1 million profit, and to James's wife that seemed a little too good to be true. However, as things worked out, I would greatly exceed my promise.

James had never bought coins like this before, and he was really interested in the process. We enjoyed a very lively conversation. James agreed not to sell the 1804 Eagle until the public could be educated about this wonderful coin, then fate intervened. I happened to acquire another client with another private plane, and our plans changed.

The gentleman I met owned a big company, and he had been collecting small-denomination U.S. coins, mainly Nickels and Quarters, and he wanted to become my silent partner. He envisioned setting up an auction company to sell rare coins, and we began with me successfully selling his collection.

Meanwhile, I found out that James had been talking to other people about his 1804 Plain-4 Eagle, and they had told him that they could sell it for $4 million. I was a little concerned that James was trying to sell the coin both without my participation and before this book came out, but I contacted my new client and we talked.

I explained the importance of this coin to my new client, extolled the rarity of the 1804 Plain-4 Eagle, and offered my opinion that over the next five years, this coin would be one of the most celebrated American coins, and that it would fetch $8 million when it was sold again. In short, I told him it was the rarest, most valuable U.S. gold coin on the market, and that it was a good buy at $5 million.

Upon hearing this, my new customer decided that this coin was indeed underpriced and so paid the $5 million asking price — and James had a $3 million profit in just a year and a half. To say the very least, James and his wife were very happy.

Now the 1804 Plain-4 Eagle has a new home and at $5 million, it has taken its rightful place in the Pantheon of American coins, but it still is not as well known as it should be both among coin collectors and the general public. This is certainly the rarest of all gold Eagles, and it is arguably the rarest American gold coin. It has a history that is unmatched in romance, and the tale of its creation is unsurpassed in the annals of numismatics. It is indeed the "King of Eagles."

AMERICA
1911

CHAPTER TWO

In the Beginning: Money in America

While trying to understand and appreciate the 1804 Plain-4 Eagle, it is perhaps best to start with a brief overview of the history of coinage in America from the earliest days to the first minting of gold coins in 1795. It is, I hope, a fascinating adventure that is really something of an outline of American history.

When America's first colonists came to these shores, they did not bring with them much money. They expected (for the most part) to grow or make what they needed and to barter for or trade the rest.

Livestock, animal pelts, tobacco, grain, and home-distilled whiskey, among other things, were often used as barter goods. In some instances, the American colonists also made use of a kind of money common to the Native Americans called "wampum" — and no, wampum is not a word made up for movies and bad fiction. It was typically two different types of beads made from two different types of shells — the periwinkle and the quahog clam.

According to Roger Williams (1603–1683), the founder of Providence and the colony of Rhode Island, six small white beads made from the periwinkle shell were worth one English penny. However, only three larger black (or bluish-black) beads made from the quahog's shell were worth an English penny. Fraud soon developed in this system, with the Native Americans dyeing white beads black and the colonists making fake beads.

As time went on, Colonial Americans began expanding their economy, and skilled workmen began leaving the farms to become artisans and craftsmen, such as cabinetmakers, silversmiths, and blacksmiths. In addition, stores began to open and both these and the makers of durable goods needed a medium of exchange — they needed good, reliable money whose value everyone understood and accepted.

This lack of hard currency was crushing the economy in the English colonies, and at one point the Massachusetts Bay Colony actually authorized the use of iron nails and musket balls as currency (the musket balls were valued at a farthing each). This inability to readily exchange goods for hard money hurt the farmers and fisherman because they could not turn what they grew or caught into cash to buy things their families needed for survival — much less for prosperity — and English money was very scarce.

As Colonial trade began to burgeon, merchants began acquiring a variety of foreign coins from such places as Portugal, Holland, France, and Spain, those that had found their way into the Colonial economy. The most important of these was perhaps the "Spanish Dollar," which was an Eight Reales ("reales" translates as "royals") coin that was minted in such places as Mexico City, Mexico, Lima, Peru, and Seville, Spain.

This Spanish Dollar was first minted in 1497 and was actually legal tender in the United States until 1857. These coins were a world currency, because Spain was an international power with an empire that literally spanned the globe. Even after the first coinage of American silver Dollars in 1794, the Spanish Dollar coin was more popular with Americans because it was more easily obtained and widely used in world commerce.

In Colonial America, the Spanish Dollar was occasionally cut into parts or bits to make change, but the use of fractional Spanish coins, such

1652 NE Sixpence (Photo courtesy of Stack's)

as the One and Two Reales, was much more common. The familiar phrase from those cheesy pirate movies — "pieces of eight" — refers to the fact that the Spanish Dollar was worth Eight Reales. Phrases such as "two bits" (i.e., Two Reales) for a Quarter Dollar still persist in our language.

THE FIRST AMERICAN MINT

In 1652, the legislature of the Massachusetts Bay Colony passed a bill that was actually an act of outright defiance of English law. The act authorized a mint to be built in Boston, where goldsmith John Hull would receive silver bullion, plate, and Spanish Dollars to be melted down, and the resulting metal would be made into coins with denominations of Threepence, Sixpence, or Twelvepence.

The mint building was erected on Hull's property, just behind his Boston home, and the first coins produced were very primitive and somewhat crude by world standards. According to the law, they were of sterling standard (925 parts of pure silver to every 1,000 parts of metal),

1652 NE Shilling (Photo courtesy of Stack's)

and they were crafted by producing small discs of silver and then hand hammering an "NE" for New England on one side and the denomination on the other — either a "XII" for Twelvepence (one Shilling), a "VI" for Sixpence, and a "III" for Threepence.

Unfortunately, these coins could be easily tampered with, and "clipping" (unscrupulous individuals would "clip" [shave] small pieces of precious metal from the coin in such a way that it might go unnoticed) and counterfeiting might have become a problem in very short order. Since the coin was worth the value of the silver it contained, this diminished the overall value of the coin, and merchants were soon wary to accept these for payment because they could easily be shortchanged.

COINS AND TREES

After about four months of making these coins, it was decided that they were unsatisfactory and that the design on them had to be more intricate in order to thwart clipping and counterfeiting. Today, these simple

1652 Willow Tree Sixpence (Photo courtesy of Stack's)

first coins are very rare, with only a few of the Threepence and Sixpence coins known to exist. The Shillings (Twelvepence) are nearly as rare.

The new coins, which were authorized by Massachusetts Bay Colony on October 19, 1652, had design elements near the outer perimeter so that clipping would not be as easily (or as unnoticeably) accomplished. The new coins had the image of what is generally called a "willow tree" in the center of the obverse, but the depiction is rather abstract, and the tree on this coin was sometimes referred to as a "palmetto tree" in the nineteenth century. Around the outer edge of the obverse is "Masathusets In," and this is enclosed in a double ring of dots. The reverse of this coin has "New England An. Dom." (for Anno Domini) around the outer edge with the date — 1652 — and the denomination in the center. Again, the values were Threepence, Sixpence, and Twelvepence.

These coins were made for some time, but there is conjecture as to exactly how long. Most experts feel that the minting of these coins stopped in either 1659 or 1660, and all were dated 1652 for a reason that will be addressed shortly. There were a number of variations in the dies used to make these pieces, and many of these coins are double or triple struck. Today, only a few dozen specimens of these coins are known to exist.

The next coins produced at the Boston Mint were relatives of the "Willow Tree" coins and are known to collectors as the "Oak Tree" coins. These came into existence around 1660, the year King Charles II came to the English throne. England had been in turmoil since the execution of Charles I in 1649, and the government in control during the so-called English Interregnum — the Protectorate of Oliver Cromwell and his son Richard — was sympathetic to the Puritan cause.

This means (among other things) that Massachusetts had actually gotten away with the coinage it began in 1652, but when Charles II assumed power, things changed dramatically — and not for the better. Charles II was livid that the colony had defied royal power and English law by minting coins, and he wanted it stopped immediately.

By that time Charles had turned his attention to Massachusetts coinage. The new Oak Tree coins were in production, and this change in design happened to be very fortuitous for the Colonial cause. Charles II summoned Sir Thomas Temple, the first agent sent by the Massachusetts General Court, to London, and Temple defended the colony rather effectively.

First he suggested that the colonies were an ignorant, backwoods bunch unaware of the law. Then he went on to say that the Oak Tree coin was actually a tribute to Charles II, and that the oak tree depicted on the coin was a reference to the tree in which the fleeing Prince Charles had hidden after the disastrous Battle of Worcester on September 3, 1651. Charles had hidden himself in an oak tree at Boscobel House to escape capture and certain death, and this tree is sometimes referred to as the "royal oak."

Charles is said to have been so touched by this "tribute" to him and his eventual triumph in ascending to the English throne that he did not order the immediate closure of the mint — but he did not authorize

1652 Oak Tree Shilling (Photo courtesy of Stack's)

further coinage either. As a result, substantial bribes were rumored to have been sent to the English Crown over the years in order to stave off closure of the Mint.

All of the original Oak Tree coins — the Threepence, Sixpence, and Twelvepence (Shilling) pieces — are dated 1652, but the Twopence coin, which was first authorized on May 7, 1662, is an exception. These coins were actually dated 1662, which makes this denomination unique among the Oak Tree coins.

Because it is the only Twopence coin made in New England, and because of its different date (1662), this Twopence coin is probably the most desired by those modern collectors interested in the Massachusetts coinage. Like the Willow Tree coins, many varieties of these Oak Tree coins were made, and it is believed that several different obverse and reverse dies were used in varying combinations during the period these coins were being manufactured. However, only one obverse and one reverse die were used to make the Twopence coins, but these dies were recut several times, producing coins that sometimes appear, to

1652 Pine Tree Shilling (Photo courtesy of Stack's)

beginning collectors, to be from different dies. The next coinage in this series is known as the "Pine Tree" coins, and although they are generally thought to have first been minted in 1667, many sources suggest that these are an outgrowth of the "Oak Tree" grouping and that precise dating is a matter of speculation. This conjecture is based on the last of the "Oak Tree" variety of coins, called "spiny branches," which actually looks very much like a pine tree.

There is some thought among coin specialists that there may actually be an evolution regarding the two types of coins, that the oak tree simply evolved into looking more like a pine tree, therefore, there is no sharply delineated time frame when the "Pine Tree" coins started being minted. These coins came in a variety of forms, with the early Shilling coins being on large, thin planchets and the later ones on smaller, thicker blanks.

The minting of these Massachusetts coins ceased sometime around 1682, but as it has been said earlier, all of the coins in this series were dated 1652 except for the "Oak Tree Twopence" coin, which was dated

1662. Why 1652? Well, colonists are said to have reasoned that if the British Crown ordered the minting of coins to be stopped at some future date, then any coin dated 1652 was earlier than the date of any stop-production order that might be issued. This meant that the colony could continue minting coins dated 1652, even if ordered to cease coining at a later date. (Some numismatists prefer an alternate theory, that the date of 1652 was kept because it was the authorizing date.)

AMERICAN COINS MADE IN ENGLAND

After this Massachusetts Bay Colony act of defiance was over, the availability of hard money continued to be a problem. In Maryland, the Lord Protector, who was Cecil Calvert, Lord Baltimore, thought it was inappropriate for the Englishmen living in his colony to be using beads (wampum) and iron objects for money, so he had silver and copper coins made in England for the colonists in Maryland to use.

Calvert thought he had the right to do this under his royal charter, and starting in 1658 or 1659, he had silver and copper coins minted in London. His assumption was understandable, since his charter had given him the unprecedented right to wage war, collect taxes, and establish Colonial nobility. His rent to the English Crown was one fifth of all the gold and silver found in Maryland, plus two "Indian" arrows delivered to Windsor castle every Easter.

The coins Calvert created were very professionally made. They were much more sophisticated and far less primitive than the coins first manufactured in Massachusetts just a few years earlier. The Shilling, Sixpence, and Fourpence coins in this series were all silver, while the Penny (or Denarium) was copper.

The silver coinage contained Lord Baltimore's portrait, values were expressed in Roman numerals, and the reverse contained Calvert's heraldic shield, with a crown above it. The Penny, which was marked "Denarium," had a crown, staffs, and banners on the obverse. This

1659 Lord Baltimore Shilling, Maryland (Photo courtesy of Stack's)

Denarium is the rarest coin of the grouping and is thought never to have been released for actual circulation.

Unfortunately for Calvert, the British government disagreed with his right to produce coins for use in the Maryland Colony. He was jailed, his coinage dies were seized, and many of the coins were confiscated. The results of this dustup are not really known, but Lord Baltimore must have prevailed, because he retained his proprietorship in Maryland until his death in 1675.

The first royally sanctioned coinage for the American colonies was authorized in 1688 by James I. At that time, John Holt was granted a franchise to produce coins of tin that could be used throughout the colonies — but in practice they were used only sparingly, if at all, as small change in the Colonial marketplaces. Most of the issued pieces were probably used in England and Ireland.

Because of their base metal content, these coins are generally referred to as "tokens," or, more specifically, "Plantation Tokens," because at the time the English public thought that their American colonies

1688 Americana Plantation Token (Photo courtesy of Stack's)

were composed of large, dispersed farming establishments, and they did not understand that there was a burgeoning urban population in the New World.

The new coin was struck in the Tower of London Mint, and it had a stated face value of one twenty-fourth of a Spanish Reale. The original worth of these coins was a little vague, with some sources saying the value worked out to being about a farthing (one fourth of an English penny). Since these coins were made essentially from pure tin, they are subject to what is called "tin pest," or sometimes "tin disease" or even "tin leprosy."

At 56 degrees Fahrenheit and below, pure tin tends to change from a silvery metal to a gray one, and it begins to turn to powder. This can be alleviated by adding small amounts of antimony and/or bismuth to the original batch of metal (and voila, you have one of the many formulas for pewter). Anyway, one of the most dramatic examples of tin pest was during Napoleon's retreat from Russia in the fall of 1812.

His troops supposedly had buttons made from tin, and as they retreated through the frigid Eastern European winter, legend has it that

1723 Rosa Americana Twopence

these buttons turned to powder and the French troops had nothing to hold their clothes together. This is a great story with graphic images of soldiers desperately trying to keep their pants from falling around their knees, but it is probably not true.

The 1688 Colonial Plantation Tokens have this same problem, and most that are found have a somewhat degraded surface. In addition, these coins were restruck in 1828 in London by coin dealer Matthew Young, who used the original iron dies. However, these dies were approximately 140 years old at the time and were rusted and defective. The restruck coins usually show these problems quite clearly.

Because the so-called Plantation Tokens had not proven very successful, it was a long time before another British entrepreneur decided to try minting coins for the American Colonial market. The next person to have a go at this was William Wood, who owned several tin and copper mines and had an "in" with King George I's mistress, the Duchess of Kendall.

Through the duchess (who had received 10,000 pounds in sterling for her trouble in brokering the deal, a huge amount of money at the time), Wood had received the right to make coins for Ireland — and as an adjunct for America as well. He got the franchise on June 16, 1722, for fourteen years, with an annual fee of 300 pounds of sterling — 100 pounds for the king and 200 pounds to the clerk comptroller. Sounds like George I got the short end of this deal!

These coins, which were known as the "Rosa Americana" because of the rose depicted on the reverse, were made from something called "Bath metal." This was composed of 75 percent copper, 23.7 percent zinc, and 0.3 percent silver, with a bit of tin and bismuth mixed in for good measure. The coins made from this material had to be struck while the metal was hot, and bubbles often formed during this process that made the surface porous and sometimes discolored.

These coins came in Twopence, Penny, and Half-Penny denominations and were distinguished by the portrait of George I on one side and a Tudor rose on the back, with the motto "Rosa Americana Utile Dulci" (the American Rose, the useful with the agreeable). Various roses were depicted, and some were crowned and some were not. In addition, on a pattern 1733 Twopence piece, minted after William Wood's death in 1730, there is a depiction of a rose bush with "Rosa: Sine: Spina" (a rose without thorns) as the motto.

The Rosa Americana coins were very lightweight, and most merchants in the colonies refused to accept them. The General Assembly of Massachusetts, due to a lack of small change, had authorized the printing of paper money in Twopence, Threepence, and Penny denominations before it knew of them. Most Rosa Americana coins are dated 1722, 1723, and 1724, and they were very much a failure.

The fascinating story of American Colonial coinage could be explored much more thoroughly, but we need to turn our attention now to coinage in America after the end of the Revolutionary War and into the years of the early federal government, which came into being in 1789.

Röſken
Bundien
Zelau

CHAPTER THREE

The Revolutionary War and Early Coinage under the Federal Government

Around the beginning of the American Revolution, money was still a big problem. Silver money was hard to acquire, and the problem was exacerbated by those who were hoarding precious metals. As early as 1729, Benjamin Franklin argued for the use of paper money, and several colonies actually issued currency to help pay their debts.

In 1775, the Second Continental Congress authorized the issuing of paper money with the value of 2 million Spanish Dollars. This measure was adopted on June 22, 1775, the day Congress received the news of the Battle of Breed's Hill (perhaps better known as the Battle of Bunker Hill).

This resolution called for the printing of 49,000 each of One, Two, Three, Four, Five, Six, Seven, and Eight Dollar notes, plus 11,800 Twenty Dollar bills (a lot of money in those days). The bills were redeemable for Spanish Milled Dollars, or the value in gold or silver. The new money was printed by the firm of Hall and Sellers on paper so thick that the British called it "the pasteboard currency of the rebels." Some of the paper was furnished by none other than Benjamin Franklin.

Congress called it "Continental currency," and by the final days of 1775, Congress had so increased the printing that $6 million in these bills had been issued. By 1779, the amount had rocketed to $240 million, and, as the saying went, this money was "not worth a Continental." In fact, by 1781, $100 in gold or silver would purchase $16,000 in Continental currency. This money was easily counterfeited, which only added to its problems.

COINAGE DURING THE REVOLUTIONARY WAR (1775–1783)

Paper money in early America proved completely inadequate and was never very popular with the people, who greatly preferred metal coins made from silver or gold. After the signing of the Declaration of Independence, the first former colony to start making coins was New Hampshire.

The coin the New Hampshire General Assembly envisioned was made from "pure copper," and the value of this coin would be 108 for every Spanish Milled Dollar — the approximate value of an English Halfpence. William Moulton was authorized to manufacture these coins, but it is thought that only a few of them were made. These 1776 coins are extremely rare. The main variety has a tree on the obverse and a harp on the reverse.

While New Hampshire was the first local government to begin minting coins after the signing of the Declaration of Independence, the new central government decided to issue coins as well. The Congress in Philadelphia thought that its new nation was about to receive large loans from France, and this, plus various other reasons, prompted it to issue the 1776 Continental Dollar.

In July 1776, fighting in the Revolutionary War had already been going on for a year, even though the Declaration of Independence was not signed until that month. The Continental Congress felt that relying

1776 Continental Dollar (Photo courtesy of Stack's)

on the currencies of other countries, as had been done in the past, might present more than a few problems, so it decided to try minting a silver Dollar for public use.

The Spanish Milled Dollar (Eight Reales) and its subdivisions (such as the Two Reales) were the standard coins of the realm, but Congress feared a shortage, and there were problems with the valuation of the Spanish coins in different areas of the country. It might be seven shillings in paper currency in one state, but nine shillings in another.

As discussed earlier, the Continental Congress had already authorized the printing of paper money, but that was not really going well, and no one liked it very much. As a symbol of the country's new nation-state status, the Continental Congress decided to mint a silver Dollar. Depreciation of the Continental paper currency doomed the idea very quickly, and the dies were used to strike pieces in brass and pewter. (It is doubtful whether these later pieces were used as coins in the marketplace, and most were probably just souvenirs.)

1777 Spanish Eight Reales, Potosi Mint (Photo courtesy of Stack's)

It is assumed that the silver coin was a "Dollar." Around the outer rim of the obverse is "Continental Currency 1776," and in the center is a sundial with the sun's rays beaming down, with the phrases "Mind Your Business" and "Fugio," or, "I Fly," meaning time flies. These are often interpreted as very Benjamin Franklin–sounding maxims.

Thirteen interlocked circles are found on the reverse, containing the name of each state, and in the center a circular "American Congress" surrounds "We Are One." It should be noted that the word "Currency" on the obverse is spelled three different ways on these coins, including "Curency" and "Currencey."

On some of these coins the inscription "EG Fecit" (i.e., "EG made it") appears, and it is thought that this is the signature of the engraver. The initials "EG" probably belong to Elisha Gallaudet of Freehold, New Jersey (some references say Philadelphia, Pennsylvania), who used a nearly identical design on the one-sixteenth Dollar of Continental paper currency. Collectors need to be aware that this coin was restruck for the 1876 Philadelphia Centennial Exposition and for other occasions.

1779 Continental Paper $35 (Photo courtesy of Stack's)

Interestingly, the first coins authorized by Congress in 1787 and bearing the phrase "United States" were based on the Continental currency design. They are generally called the "Fugio Cents" although, as recently noted by Eric Newman, these should be called the "Fugio Coppers," as their copper content was far below the standard for the authorized Cent. James Jarvis was supposed to produce 300 tons of these coins, but he failed to deliver the full amount and was forced to flee to avoid imprisonment.

COINAGE AFTER THE END OF THE REVOLUTIONARY WAR

After the end of the Revolutionary War, the money problems persisted until federal coinage started appearing in 1793. During the mid- to late-eighteenth century, Vermont felt as though it was not getting any respect from its neighbors — New York and New Hampshire. New York claimed the Vermont territory, as did New Hampshire, and to escape

1787 Fugio Copper Coin (Photo courtesy of Stack's)

the grasp of its land-hungry neighbors, Vermont declared itself an independent republic on January 15, 1777. It retained this status until it became the fourteenth state on March 4, 1791.

In June 1785, the House of Representatives of the Freemen of Vermont and the Governor's Council (the name given to the upper house of the Vermont Legislature at that time) agreed to allow Reuben Harmon Jr. to establish a mint and to produce copper coins that were to weigh one third of a troy ounce (this weight was soon lowered to four pennyweights and fifteen grains). This made Vermont the first governmental entity associated with the new United States of America to mint coins.

Harmon's new mint was located beside the Millbrook stream in Rupert, Vermont, and it was reportedly a small building, just 16 by 18 feet. Harmon had the dream and the copper to make his mint profitable, but he did not have the skill that was required to make the dies necessary to produce coins.

For this, Harmon hired the famous New York City silversmithing firm that consisted of Daniel Van Voorhis and William Coley, and it is

1785 Vermont Cent (Photo courtesy of Stack's)

actually thought that Coley did the work because he later moved to Vermont to help Harmon with his mint. The initial design Coley made featured the image of the sun rising over the Green Mountains with the representation of a plow in the foreground, and it is considered by many a beautiful and thoroughly "American" image.

There were three different inscriptions, but they were all variations of "Res Publica Vermontensium" (the "Republic of Vermont"). On the reverse was an all-seeing eye (the Eye of Providence), surrounded by rays and thirteen stars, with the motto "Stella Quarta Decima," or "The Fourteenth Star," suggesting that Vermont wanted to join with the other thirteen states in the American Confederation.

These coins were produced from 1785 to 1788, and they came in a wide range of variations. In 1787 the reverse design was changed to an image that can only be identified as "Britannia," with a man wearing a laurel wreath in his hair as though he were a conquering Roman ruler. This figure is often identified as George III, which seems at first consideration to be a rather incongruous idea. The inscriptions were also changed to "Auctoritate Vermontensium" (by the authority of Vermont), and INDE: ET: LIB (Independence and Liberty).

Why the change? It is speculated that the look of the coin may have been changed so that it more closely resembled the English copper Halfpenny coinage. This may have been done to improve consumer acceptance of the coins by making them look like the standard English copper coins that consumers had long been accustomed to using and accepting. This theory may have no basis in actual fact, but it is an intriguing speculation.

The Harmon mint closed early in 1789, and much of the equipment was sent to Thomas Machin's mill in Newburgh, New York, where more Vermont coppers were manufactured for a short time. Numismatic scholar Kenneth Bressett has stated that no more than 5,000 of these coins have survived to the present day.

BRASHER DOUBLOONS

As has been previously suggested, coins made in early America were most often crafted from copper, with only a few made in silver, brass, and pewter. There was, however, one gold coinage that is considered the first made in the United States.

Ephraim Brasher was a noted New York City gold and silversmith who just happened to live next to George Washington at 5 Cherry Street, when the U.S. capital was New York City. Washington was a customer of Brasher's, and Brasher is thought to have been a great admirer of the "Father of Our Country."

Brasher was also in the assay business, and customers would bring him their foreign gold coins to be evaluated as to their weight and purity. After this was done, Brasher would stamp the genuine coins with his "EB" hallmark to attest to the fact that it was as it should be.

There is some debate as to why Brasher decided to make a gold coin that was about the size of a Spanish gold Doubloon. It is said that

1787 Brasher Doubloon

he had no intention of making these coins for circulation but rather was proposing a model for later coinage done by the U.S. government.

Brasher's coin contained 26.6 grams of gold, which was 91.7 percent pure. The obverse of this coin depicts the New York State seal with the sun rising above a mountain (not unlike the Vermont coin, discussed earlier) and a seal with "Brasher" below it. The circular legend on the obverse has "Nova Eboraca Columbia Excelsior." *Nova Eboraca* is Latin for New York. On the reverse of this coin is a representation of an eagle surrounded by the motto "E Pluribus Unum" (out of many, one), which would later become the familiar motto found on our money to this day. There was also a date — 1787 — and Ephraim Brasher's "EB" hallmark. There are seven known examples of the Brasher Doubloon. Six have the hallmark on the wing, while the seventh has the mark on the shield located on the eagle's breast.

Two of these — one with the EB hallmark on the wing and the other with the hallmark on the breast (often called the "Dupont specimen") — were sold by Heritage Galleries in recent years, with each bringing $3 million! These coins have been featured in several Hollywood movies, including a 1947 film noir taken from the Raymond Chandler story "The Brasher Doubloon."

THE NEW FEDERAL MINT

The Coinage Act of April 1792 was to create a U.S. Mint that would soon be placed under the Department of State. President George Washington appointed David Rittenhouse of Philadelphia the first director of the new mint on April 14, 1792. Rittenhouse had to be persuaded to take the new job because he was in very poor health. He left the post in 1795 and died in 1796.

Rittenhouse must have been a man after Benjamin Franklin's own heart. He was something of a Renaissance man — an astronomer, an inventor, a maker of scientific instruments, a clock maker, a surveyor, a mathematician, and a politician. Although he received an honorary master of science degree from the College of Pennsylvania, Rittenhouse was a self-taught genius who was born on April 8, 1732, in Rittenhousetown (also called "Paper Mill Run"), Pennsylvania, located near Philadelphia.

At age nineteen, Rittenhouse established a scientific instrument shop on his father's farm, where he built orreries (working mechanical models of the solar system), and he was one of the first Americans to build a telescope. As a surveyor he, along with Andrew Ellicott, finished the survey of the legendary Mason-Dixon line, which delineated some of the borders of Pennsylvania, Maryland, Delaware, and Virginia (now West Virginia).

Charles Mason and Jeremiah Dixon's survey (1763–1767) had been stopped by Native Americans, but in 1784, Rittenhouse and Ellicott extended it to the southwest corner of Pennsylvania, five degrees' longitude from the Delaware River. Other surveyors would complete the job to the Ohio River. Rittenhouse built an observatory, where he discovered the atmosphere of Venus; invented the metallic thermometer; and was treasurer of the state of Pennsylvania from 1779 to 1787.

Mint Director David Rittenhouse

After giving it some thought, Rittenhouse suggested a site for the new mint, a former distillery on North 7th Street, plus an adjoining lot on Filbert Street. Henry Voight was employed to be the chief coiner, but Thomas Jefferson (the then secretary of state, and Rittenhouse's boss) tried to find a more experienced craftsman in Europe, and Voight's job was considered temporary.

Fortunately for Voight, who had actually worked in a German mint, Jefferson failed in his European efforts, and Voight retained his job until his death in February 1814. It was Voight who was in charge when the 1804 Crosslet-4 Eagle was originally coined. It was also Voight who designed some of the early coins produced by the new mint, especially the 1793 Chain and Wreath Cents.

Demolition of the old distillery began on July 19, and by July 30, building materials were on site and the foundation was being laid. The first coins were minted in July 1792, long before the buildings were complete; these were the well-known Half "Dismes." At about the same time, pattern Cents and Dismes (Dimes) were struck. These coins were actually minted in John Harper's basement, on 6th and Cherry Streets, not far from the future mint building. Harper had made this space available at Rittenhouse's request, and it was used until the new mint was ready for occupancy.

1792 Half Disme (Photo courtesy of Eel River Collection)

George Washington was particularly interested in the beginning of American coinage in order to aid commerce and the economy, and, as has been reported, he and Martha supposedly contributed their silverware (sometimes said to be a tea set, other times flatware) for this purpose. There is no actual record of this having occurred, but Walter Breen observed in a pamphlet he wrote in the 1950s that upon Washington's death in 1799, he owned no sterling silver pieces of any kind — just items made from Sheffield plate (a thin sheet of silver bonded by heat to a much thicker sheet of copper).

Breen reasoned that a man of Washington's wealth and position should have had some household objects made from sterling silver and suggested that this gave credence to the old story about the Washington silver having been melted done down to make some of the first U.S. coins.

There is some disagreement about whether these first coins were meant for circulation or were just trial pieces (called "pattern" coins). Documentary evidence revealed that 1,500 of the Half Dismes were made, but this seems to be quite a lot for pieces that were not meant for any kind of distribution. Today, most experts believe that these coins were regular issues and were indeed circulated.

Of all the coins struck by the United States in 1792, the first and the most important is probably the 1792 Half Disme. It is speculated that this coin was probably designed by Robert Birch (see discussion of the Birch Cent that follows), but no one is completely sure about this. In fact, no one is entirely sure that Birch's first name was Robert, and some say the designer was actually William Russell Birch, a British engraver who arrived in the United States around this time.

This coin was made from metal that many collectors might describe as "coin silver," and it was 89.24 percent silver and 10.76 percent copper. Those interested in American silver usually say that "coin silver" is 90 percent pure silver and 10 percent copper, but everyone acknowledges that these proportions do vary.

The law passed on April 2, 1792, required this coin to be decorated with "a device emblematic of liberty" (i.e., the "Goddess of Liberty"). The legend persists that the image chosen was that of Martha Washington, but this is open to both conjecture and much doubt. The reverse of this coin has a most unusual-looking eagle in flight and an abbreviated motto for "Liberty Parent of Science and Industry" (LIB. PAR. OF SCIENCE & INDUSTRY).

The large pattern Cent coin that was made is referred to as the "Birch Cent," because it is signed "Birch" on the truncation (lower edge) of the bust; Robert Birch is thought by some to have created the design, although others prefer William Russell Birch. It has been speculated that Birch was an engraver who submitted a pattern for a Cent coin in 1791 or 1792, and that Rittenhouse chose him to create the dies for the new Cent and Half Disme.

On the front of this Cent coin is a portrait of the "Goddess of Liberty" and, again, it has been speculated that this image is based on a representation of Martha Washington taken not from life but from an

1792 Birch Cent (Photo courtesy of Professional Coin Grading Service, Inc.)

oil portrait. This is somewhat ironic, because President Washington had refused to allow his portrait to appear on the new coinage.

The back of the Birch Cent was decorated with a wreath surrounded by "United States of America," with "One Cent" in the center of the wreath and 1/100 below. The pattern Cent coins were made from copper, but a white metal specimen exists from a variant reverse die. The production of these Birch Cents failed, because the mint did not have sufficient copper to produce enough coins.

The rising price of copper in late 1792 forced the government to consider reducing the weight of the Cent and Half Cent coins; it was then suggested that they be made from a type of metal called "billon," an alloy of silver with a base metal — generally copper — where the amount of silver is less than half the weight. Copper is the major metal in the composition, which can be as low as 2 percent silver or as high as 49 percent.

Billon has been used since ancient times, and it was familiar to Voight because it was used in Germany, where Voight had served in the

1793 Chain Cent (Photo courtesy of Stack's)

Saxe-Gotha Mint. The word *billon* is said to have been taken from the Middle French *bille*, for a small log, or from the Latin *billo*, for a coin containing copper or a unit of payment. The later derivation seems more to the point.

As a test, some 1792 small size Cents were made in December with a small plug of silver in the center, but there were technical difficulties, and this experiment was soon abandoned. Using the same dies, which had been engraved by Chief Coiner Voight, planchets with a billon mixture were coined shortly afterward. The Cent coins with the small silver plugs are reportedly the first coins actually struck in the new mint building, which was ready for occupancy in September 1792.

The idea was to make a Cent coin that was actually worth one cent. Therefore, the silver plug contained metal that was valued at three fourths of a cent and was surrounded by copper that was valued at one fourth of a cent. This bit of manipulation was just an experiment and was very short-lived.

As a result of a request by Mint Director Rittenhouse, on January 14,

1793 Wreath Cent (Photo courtesy of Stack's)

1793, Congress reduced the weight of copper used in Cent coins, which cleared the way for their earnest striking. The first 1793 Cent had an image of a female bust with flowing, almost windswept, hair on the obverse with the word "Liberty" above and the date 1793 below. On the reverse, "United States of America" appeared around the outside, surrounding a chain of fifteen links arranged in a circle with "One Cent" inside over the fraction 1/100.

Unfortunately, this was not a popular coin, because the figure of Liberty appeared to be fleeing from something, and the chain on the back, instead of being a symbol for the then fifteen states, reminded some of slavery and bondage. Symbolically, this new coin had some really serious but unintended problems.

The coin was quickly redesigned, and Liberty was more boldly depicted, but she still had flowing hair. On the reverse, the circle of chain links was replaced with a laurel wreath, but still, this coin was not very popular with American consumers.

1793 Liberty Cap Cent (Photo courtesy of Stack's)

A second redesign, made in early September 1793 by Joseph Wright, was more enduring; it featured Liberty with hair that is freely flowing, but not quite so windswept. Over her shoulder Liberty is carrying a staff that has a liberty cap on the end. This is clearly visible if a close and careful look is taken, but a cursory glance at this new design gives the impression that Liberty has a big bow in her hair to hold back the formerly unruly locks.

We have been discussing the beginnings of the U.S. Mint in Philadelphia and the early coins that were made there, but what about gold coins? What is their history around the world, when were they first minted in the United States, and why?

ONE SHILLING
E·PLURIBUS·UNUM
1882
SHILLING
CANADA ONE CENT 1920

CHAPTER FOUR

Gold Coins around the World

There has never been anything quite like gold. It creates wealth, causes wars, and prompts nations to grow and expand. It is a commodity hotly desired by both men and women. It is also one of the metals from which coins of the highest value have been minted for centuries.

The chemical symbol for gold is Au, which is derived from the Latin word *aurum*, which means "shining dawn." Gold is thought to have been the first metal worked by man in prehistoric times. It was valued both for its ornamental value and for its use in rituals. It was one of the legendary gifts of the Magi, and it was sometimes even used as a medicine, based on the theory that something so beautiful and rare had to be good for you if taken internally.

The first encounters of man and gold are lost to history but probably occurred when shiny pebbles of exceptional color and texture were found glistening in streams. Bits of gold have been found in caves occupied by Paleolithic man as far back as 40,000 B.C., but it would be several thousand years before jewelry and coins would be crafted from this precious and remarkable substance.

During the second millennium B.C., it is asserted by French historian Fernand Braudel (1902–1985) that gold and silver were the "lifeblood of Mediterranean trade," but these metals were not in the form of coins. They were used as ingots that could be divided or cut into smaller chunks or as wire. Gold wire was relatively easy to make, because gold is so malleable and ductile that it can be drawn into a thread so fine that it can be used for embroidery.

Gold decorative objects first appeared in Eastern Europe around 3000 B.C., and in Southern Iraq, gold jewelry started being made around the same date. The Chinese started using small squares of gold as a form of monetary exchange around 1090 B.C., but the first actual coinage of precious metals is thought to have been minted around 650 B.C. in Lydia, which was an ancient country located in present-day Eastern Turkey (in Asia).

Lydia was situated in Anatolia, a peninsula of land in western Asia Minor that is bracketed by the Black Sea and the Mediterranean and comprises the modern Turkish provinces of Izmir and Manisa. These first coins were actually made from "electrum," which is a naturally occurring substance composed of approximately 70 to 90 percent gold, the rest being silver and other metals, including copper. The ancients generally found electrum in streams.

While the gold composition in naturally occurring electrum was generally 70 to 90 percent, these ancient Lydian coins were about 45 to 55 percent gold, and it was not until around 560 B.C. that the Lydians learned to separate the gold from the silver and other metals. According to Greek historian Herodotus, the coins were called "Staters," which meant "standard," and generally had the image of a lion on the front (the symbol of the Lydian king) with a punch or seal on the back.

A variety of these coins existed. One Stater was composed of about 14.1 grams of electrum. The Stater was divided into smaller coins with one-third Stater being called a "Trite" and one-sixth Stater a "Hekte." The denominations went down to one ninety-sixth, which had about

Electrum Stater of Lydia, about 650 B.C.

.015 gram of electrum. Incidentally, a Stater was approximately the amount a Lydian soldier earned in one month.

Coinage spread to the Greek city-states, where some governmental entities favored silver coins and others preferred gold. Silver was predominant until King Philip II of Macedon acquired both gold and silver mines in what was then called Thrace, now Bulgaria.

Philip's son, Alexander the Great, plundered more than 700,000 troy ounces of gold during his military conquest of Persia and made gold coinage the norm for paying soldiers as well as covering other military expenses; they featured the visage of Greek deity Athena instead of representations of lions, bulls, or rams. Unlike the gold, however, Alexander's portrait did appear on his silver coinage.

The use of an image of a ram on gold coins is interesting, because it is (at least in part and according to some) a reference to the Golden Fleece so famous in Greek mythology concerning Jason and the Argonauts. "Golden Fleece" is actually a reference to a way of mining gold by placing a sheep's or ram's fleece — sometimes attached to a wooden

Aureus of Hadrian, A.D. 119 (Photo courtesy of Stack's)

frame — into a gold-bearing stream. As the water flows over the pelt, gold gets caught in the fleece. After a time, the fleece is removed from the stream and hung in a tree to dry. When this drying process is complete, the gold is either combed or shaken out.

Other interpretations of the phrase "Golden Fleece" have been advanced by scholars, with some saying it refers to a particular breed of sheep, others to royal power, and still others to the sun reflecting off of the ocean. However, this type of mining is first known to have been done in Georgia (once part of the Soviet Union) in the fifth century B.C., and this is a bit late for the Jason and the Argonauts story, which was known to Homer in the eighth century B.C.

After the Greeks, the Romans minted vast quantities of gold coins that were used by traders, government administrators, and, perhaps most importantly, to pay legionnaires. The standard Roman gold coin was the Aureus, which was made from nearly pure metal and weighed about 7.3 grams, or slightly less than one-quarter troy ounce.

The Aureus was issued only occasionally before Julius Caesar came to power, but Caesar had it struck frequently, and millions of gold coins were minted over the next several centuries. There were other denominations besides the Aureus. Emperor Constantine, for example, introduced a smaller gold coin called the "Solidus" in A.D. 309, which weighed 4.5 grams.

Solidus means solid in Latin and from the name of this coin, the word *soldier* is derived, because soldiers were often paid with this type of money. Roman coinage brought a kind of economic unity to Europe, but after the Western Roman Empire fell in 476, gold coins would not be minted to any large amounts in Western Europe for more than 1,000 years.

The Solidus, which was called a "Nomisma" in Greek, continued to be minted in the Eastern Roman or Byzantine Empire until the tenth century. The Byzantine Empire ceased to exist in 1453, but in the meantime it struck other gold and electrum coins of varying weights and descriptions. During the Middle Ages, Europeans often called these and similar coins "Bezants," because they came from the Byzantine Empire. Many of these gold coins were brought back to Western Europe by the Crusaders returning from the wars in the Holy Land.

In the thirteenth century, two Italian city-states began minting gold coins that became significant to the Western world's economy. The first was the Florentine "Florin" and the second was the Venetian "Ducat." The gold Florin was minted between 1252 and 1523 and contained about 3.5 grams of nearly pure metal. During the fourteenth century, numerous European governments minted their own version of the Florin, the most important of these being the Hungarian "Forint."

The gold Ducat is thought to have been coined first by Roger II of Sicily in 1150. The motto on the coin read "Sit tibi, Christe, datus, quem tu regis iste ducatus," or "O Christ, let this duchy which you rule be dedicated to you." The name of this coin was derived from the last word in this motto, *ducatus*, which of course means "duchy," a reference to a territory ruled by a duke or duchess.

The Ducat was first minted by the Republic of Venice in 1284 and was called the "Zecchino." It was a very popular coin throughout Europe during the Middle Ages and even into the middle of the nineteenth century, and it is still minted today by the Netherlands and the Czech Republic as a gold bullion coin. However, most European coins of the past 1,000 years have been made from either silver or copper, not from gold.

The settlement of the New World began in earnest during the sixteenth century, and one of the most pressing reasons for settling this part of the world was the desire to find quantities of gold. An abundance of gold was discovered, and eventually Spanish mints were established as early as 1536 in several cities, including Sante Fe de Bogota, Colombia, Mexico City, and Lima, Peru. New World gold was also turned into coins in Seville, Spain.

THE BEGINNING OF GOLD COINS IN THE UNITED STATES

Most coins used in the New World, like in Europe, were made from silver or copper. In the United States, official national coinage did not begin until after the ratification of the Constitution, which was completed in September 1787, but the new government did not begin operations until April 1789. On September 2, 1789, the Treasury Department was created, and it is now the second oldest department in the new federal government.

The first secretary of the treasury was Alexander Hamilton, who was nominated by President Washington on September 11, 1789. He was confirmed by the U.S. Senate on the same day and served in this capacity until early 1795. In January 1791, Hamilton submitted his "Report on the Subject of a Mint" to Congress, and in early March of that year, Congress passed a resolution authorizing the president to take the necessary steps to create a mint.

President Washington found the congressional resolution inadequate and pointedly asked the solons for formal legislation. In April 1792, Congress passed a comprehensive law creating a national mint "at the seat of government of the United States" (Philadelphia), where coins of gold, silver, and copper would be made. The gold coins would be Eagles ($10), Half Eagles ($5), and Quarter Eagles ($2.50). The silver coins would be Dollars, Half Dollars, Quarter Dollars, Dismes (Dimes), and Half Dismes. The copper coins were Cents and Half Cents. (The official spelling of Disme was changed in January 1837 to Dime.)

The Philadelphia Mint was the first building constructed under the new Constitution, and its first director was David Rittenhouse. In 1792, Congress approved the purchase of no more than 150 tons of copper to be coined at the new mint.

The first gold coins turned out by the U.S. Mint in Philadelphia were not struck until July 1795. This book is about the story — the romance, really — of one of these gold coins that was produced in the 1830s, one of the rarest of all U.S. coins.

CHAPTER FIVE

An Overview of American Gold Coins

United States currency and coinage were based on the decimal system. Ten One-Cent pieces made one Dime, ten Dimes made one Dollar, and ten Dollars made one Eagle. Eagles are gold coins; in addition to the $10 denomination, they can be found as Quarter Eagles, worth $2.50, Half Eagles, worth $5, and Double Eagles, worth $20.

Other American gold coins include the gold Dollar, first minted in 1849, the Three-Dollar gold piece, first minted in 1854, and the "Stella," which is a very rare Four-Dollar gold piece, minted only in 1879 and 1880. The Stella, however, was actually a pattern and never authorized to be struck for public use. In addition, during the 1850s it was proposed that a $100 gold piece be minted or a coin worth ten Eagles. This coin was to be called a "Union" (or a "Half Union," for a $50 piece), but it was never struck for commercial use. In June 1795, David Rittenhouse resigned as director of the U.S. Mint and was replaced by Henry William DeSaussure (1763–1839), a lawyer and jurist from South Carolina who had become a political leader in the Federalist Party after the Revolutionary War.

DeSaussure was appointed by President Washington, and he immediately set about producing coins made from gold. He assumed

U.S. Mint Director Henry William DeSaussure

his duties on July 9, 1795, and barely three weeks later, on July 31, he oversaw the minting of the first Half Eagles. Mint records show that 744 examples of the Half Eagle were minted that day, plus one specimen for assay purposes. This is considered the birthday of U.S. gold coinage.

DeSaussure is often given credit for beginning gold coinage in the United States, but it is fairer to say that he expedited the preparations that Rittenhouse had begun. Shortly before he left the Mint, Rittenhouse had assigned engraver Robert Scot the task of executing the dies for the Half Eagle, and by the time DeSaussure had arrived, the process was well in hand.

DeSaussure's tenure at the Mint was short lived, and he left in October 1795 because his family was concerned about the unhealthy climate in Philadelphia. At the time, Philadelphia was the second-largest city in the United States, but it was still suffering from English occupation and destruction during the years of the Revolutionary War.

Even more to the point were the annual outbreaks of yellow fever in the city, which on more than one occasion caused the Mint to shut down during the late summer and early autumn months. The residents of Philadelphia who could afford to fled to the countryside during these dangerous outbreaks, and DeSaussure left his post because of concerns for his physical health and safety. He accomplished a great deal though during his short tenure, and George Washington sent him a letter noting his (Washington's) "entire satisfaction" with the way DeSaussure carried out his responsibilities. DeSaussure was replaced by Elias Boudinot (1740–1821), who would serve in the post for ten years.

At the time of the first minting of gold coins and for decades thereafter, the U.S. Mint struck gold coins only on depositors' accounts, which meant that it produced gold coins only when banks or individuals provided the gold for conversion into coinage. For example, 400 of the first $10 gold pieces (or Eagles) were delivered to the Bank of Pennsylvania, which had furnished the precious metal for their production.

There is a long-standing legend that U.S. Mint Director DeSaussure hand-delivered 100 Eagles to President Washington because the Father of Our Country was keenly interested in the production of gold coins to help our country in its worldwide commercial endeavors. It has been said that President Washington wanted gold coinage to begin before his term in office ended in 1797, and DeSaussure met that goal with time to spare.

The truth of the legend of the 100 gold Eagles delivered to President Washington has been disputed and it is considered by most an unfounded myth. One reason this story is doubted is that in order for Washington to have received these gold coins, he would have had to deposit that amount of gold with the Mint, and there is no record of this having happened unless it was done through a bank. In addition, this was a lot of money in the late eighteenth century (equivalent to about three years' wages for the average working man), and it is doubtful that Washington would have wanted to tie up that much of his own financial resources.

However, it is possible that the first president wanted to use these gold coins as presentation pieces and therefore arranged to have them made at the U.S. Mint. This supposition is somewhat borne out by the fact that many surviving 1795 gold Eagles have an almost Prooflike surface and are in excellent condition. This lends some credibility to the story that Washington might have used them for presentation purposes.

The first U.S. Mint (1792–1833) as it appeared in 1854

THE FIRST HALF EAGLES

As has already been said, the first gold coin minted by the U.S. government at the new Philadelphia Mint was the Half Eagle ($5 value). The beginning of coinage using both gold and silver had been delayed because a large bond was required of Mint officials before such coins could be struck.

The original Mint Act of April 1792 required the assayer and chief coiner to each post a bond of $10,000, an astronomical sum at that time. Neither official could meet this requirement, so the beginning of gold and silver coinage had to wait until the issue could be resolved.

In late 1793, at the request of U.S. Mint Director Rittenhouse, Thomas Jefferson, who was secretary of state at the time and the Cabinet officer overseeing the Mint, appealed to Congress to lower the bond. This impediment was resolved on March 3, 1794, when the bond for the assayer was lowered to $1,000 and for the chief coiner to $5,000. This cleared the way for the Mint to begin turning out silver coins, but gold coins had to wait until 1795.

Five dollars does not seem like very much money to us today, but in the late eighteenth century the Half Eagle was not a coin that most people carried around in their pockets when they went out shopping for their "daily bread." It was just too much money for the average person to have casually, and most of the Half Eagles were used as bullion — meaning that businesses and institutions employed them in their transactions, with many being used in international exchange. Because of this and a number of other factors, many of these coins, over time, ended up being melted down.

There was no denomination delineated on either the obverse or the reverse of these first Half Eagle coins, which may seem strange to us today. But the merchants and the bankers who would be using this coin were much more concerned with the weight of the precious metal than a stated face value. (Even though no denomination appeared on the gold coins at this time, those who handled such pieces were well aware of the value in dollars.)

The first Half Eagles were made from metal that was 91.67 percent gold and 8.33 percent copper and silver. They have a diameter of approximately 25 millimeters and contain about 8.75 grams of gold. The first gold deposited by Moses Brown of Boston — 128 ounces — arrived at the Mint in mid-February 1795, and this was followed by several small deposits. In due course, this bullion was turned into coins. The first Half Eagles — 744 of them — were delivered on July 31, 1795, and another batch of 520 pieces was delivered less than two weeks later, on August 11.

The designer of the 1795 Half Eagle was Robert Scot, who had been appointed Chief Engraver at the Mint on November 23, 1793. Scot had engraved plates to make paper currency during the Revolutionary War, but his experience with making dies for coins was limited. Some coin specialists today question his abilities, but the other possible candidates for the post had considerably less ability.

Scot's design for the Half Eagle contained the image of the "Goddess of Liberty" facing right on the front, wearing a cap surrounded with the word "Liberty," a number of stars, and the date. On the reverse was an eagle clutching a victory wreath in its beak and surrounded with the words "United States of America." The eagle is depicted standing on a branch with leaves. This design is generally called the "Capped Bust Liberty."

1795 Half Eagle (Photo courtesy of Stack's)

The design of the eagle allegedly is based on one found on a Roman cameo, but it turned out to be very unpopular, because the eagle was thought to be somewhat anemic and "scrawny," not the powerful bird that almost everyone of the day visualized as the triumphant symbol of the United States.

In order to increase the acceptance of the gold coinage, Director Elias Boudinot requested that Scot design a new eagle, one based on the Great Seal of the United States, for the Quarter Eagle first struck in late 1796. It is called a "Heraldic Eagle" because it is part of the armorial emblem of the United States and is depicted with wings "displayed" supporting the nation's shield that is emblazoned with stripes.

In heraldry, the eagle is associated with immortality, courage, and far-sightedness, and it is a messenger of the highest gods, particularly Zeus, Jupiter, and Odin. On the coin, the head of this eagle is surrounded with stars, and there is a banner in the beak that reads "E Pluribus Unum" (Out of Many, One). Interestingly, Scot did not change the Eagle ($10 gold piece) design until 1797. The Heraldic Eagle was added to

1802 Half Eagle, Overdate: 1802/1 (Photo courtesy of Stack's)

the Half Eagle in 1798, a date that is sometimes overlooked because the date 1795 also exists with this reverse.

One issue that needs to be discussed is the Mint's use of old dies when making coins during the early years of its existence. This will be important later on in the main discussion of the 1804 Plain-4 Eagle, which is the subject of this book. Making new dies was very expensive, and during its fledgling days, the Mint was not generating a great deal of revenue with its production of coins.

The overhead was relatively high, and the cost of making new dies was prohibitive, so any die that was still viable would continue to be used until it was worn out. In other words, the Mint reused dies with past years' dates on them with some regularity. It is thought by many numismatists, for example, that Half Eagle dies with a 1795 date continued to be used well into 1796.

The Mint had to practice frugality, and if a die was not worn out, then it might be used again, even if the actual date and the date on the coin did not coincide. This is clearly demonstrated by the fact that Half

Eagles dated 1795 can be found with large "heraldic" eagles on the reverse, and this reverse design for the Half Eagle did not exist until 1798. What must have happened is that a 1795 obverse die was found that was still in good condition, and thus it was used with a reverse that was not in existence until three years after the date on the face of the coin.

THE FIRST EAGLES

In September 1795, soon to be retired Mint Director Henry William DeSaussure reportedly curtailed the production of Half Eagles in order to concentrate on the production of Eagles ($10 gold pieces). This was to be the largest-denomination U.S. coin in circulation until 1850, when the first Double Eagle ($20 gold piece) was minted for circulation.

Like the Half Eagle, the design and dies for the Eagle coins were created by Robert Scot. They were just a larger version of the Half Eagle, with a capped bust of Liberty on the obverse and an eagle clutching a victory wreath in its beak while standing on a branch. Like the Half Eagle, it was 91.67 percent pure gold and 8.33 percent copper and silver. The Eagle weighed 17.5 grams (exactly double the weight of the Half Eagle) and had a diameter of around 33 millimeters.

Although most numismatists think that the alloy for gold coinage was pure copper, this was not true. The law permitted silver to be included in the alloy to add a certain beauty to the coins, and this was general practice at U.S. mints in the eighteenth and nineteenth centuries.

Most 1795 Eagles have the eagle on the reverse perched on a branch that has thirteen leaves, but some very rare examples have only nine leaves, which are very desirable from a collector's point of view. It is thought that there were less than 1,000 made of the nine-leaf variety, and few of these have survived over the years.

In 1797 the "Heraldic" Eagle design made its appearance on Eagle coins, and coins minted in that year can be found with either the so-

1795 Eagle (Photo courtesy of Stack's)

called small eagle or the Heraldic Eagle. This brings us to the 1798 over 97 Eagle coins, and while the 1795 Eagle with nine leaves is truly a rarity, the 1798 over 97 Eagle, which has seven stars on the left side of the obverse and six on the right, is considered by some to be rarer still. (The figure "8" was punched into the die over the second figure "7" in the date, which created an "overdate.")

This 1798 over 97 coin can be found in two configurations. The more common has the capped bust of liberty with nine stars to the left of the word "Liberty" and four stars to the right. Both of these are rather rare, but the nine-four star combination is more commonly found than the seven-six configuration, which is a real prize for the collector who happens to own one. Some consider this 1798 over 97 Eagle with the seven-six star configuration the "key date" among the early Eagles; fewer than twenty-five specimens are known to exist.

The 1799 Eagle, on the other hand, is a beautiful, well-struck coin that is the most plentiful of the late eighteenth-century Eagles. Reportedly, more than 37,000 of these were made, which far exceeds the production of the other Eagles made in the 1790s. The mintage of Eagles in 1800 dropped dramatically to around 6,000, but it is believed that the 1800 dated dies were also used in early 1801.

The next year, the mintage for the 1801 Eagle exceeded the number made of the 1799 Eagle, and this is the most commonly found Eagle of this early era. Reportedly, 44,344 were made (which included 15,090 pieces struck in 1802 with dies of 1801), but today probably less than 1,000 are known to exist. The coinage of Eagles in 1803, 8,979 pieces, probably carried that year's date, but it is also believed that the 1803 dies were used for several thousand pieces in 1804.

An interesting rarity exists among the Eagles dated 1803. Most of these have thirteen stars on the reverse, but some have a tiny fourteenth star that can be spotted hidden in the cloud below "F" in the word "OF" in "United States of America." This type of error was caused by an inattentive workman who miscounted the number of stars already punched into the die.

The year 1804 was the last year Eagles were struck until 1838. These coins had "Crosslet" 4's in their date, which differs from the "4's" found on the four gold 1804 Eagles that were minted during the period 1834–1835 for special diplomatic purposes. The word "Crosslet" simply means that the number 4 had a small, perpendicular line at the end of the crossbar that transected the upright in the numeral. The "Plain-4's" found on the Eagles made for presentation purposes during the period 1834–1835 do not have this feature. It is a very small detail, but it is one that can make all the difference in the world to serious collectors.

The mintage of Eagles in 1804 was 9,795 pieces, but researchers believe that part of this coinage (more than 6,000 pieces) was dated 1803. The generally accepted figure for Eagles dated 1804 is 3,757, which accounts for the well-known rarity of this issue.

QUARTER EAGLES

The minting of Quarter Eagle coins (one quarter of a $10 Eagle, or $2.50) did not begin until 1796. These coins, like the Half Eagle and the Eagle before it, were designed by Robert Scot, who used the image of a capped bust of Liberty facing right with the word "Liberty" above and the date below on the obverse and a Heraldic Eagle with a shield on the reverse.

The first obverse die for the 1796 Quarter Eagle did not have stars surrounding the head of Liberty, but a later die that same year did add the stars. The revised 1796 design was then kept in place until this type was last struck in 1807. The coins — like the other gold coins of this era — were 91.67 percent pure gold and 8.33 percent copper and silver. The Quarter Eagle had an overall weight, including the alloy, of 67.5 grains, or 4.37 grams, and was approximately 20 millimeters in diameter (the size did vary just a bit).

Reportedly, only 963 of the 1796 Quarter Eagles were made without stars on the obverse, and 432 of the specimens with stars. Both of these coins are now exceedingly rare due to low mintage numbers and later melting, but the Quarter Eagle without stars is most desirable to collectors, even though more than twice as many of these unstarred coins were originally minted. The desirability is due to the fact that this particular design (without stars on the obverse) is seen only for 1796.

In 1808, this coin was redesigned, with the figure now facing left and wearing a different cap. Liberty's face was restructured to look more feminine, and her hair was curlier. Also, the star pattern on the obverse of the 1808 Quarter Eagle did not extend over Liberty's head. John Reich was the designer of this new coin, and he also created a new rendition of the eagle for the back that showed a bird with a more elongated head and neck.

1796 Quarter Eagle, No Stars (Photo courtesy of Stack's)

This coin was made for only one year, and after 1808, the Quarter Eagle was not made again until 1821. When it was reintroduced, the star pattern surrounded the bust of Liberty and extended over her head, and the new diameter was 18.5 millimeters, but the coin contained as much gold as it had in 1808.

In 1834, the purity and weight of this and other U.S. gold coins were altered, because the international ratio between gold and silver was no longer 15 to 1, as it had been in 1792. This meant that it was profitable to melt down the coins and sell the metal in Europe. In other words, by the 1830s, there was more than $2.50 of gold in the Quarter Eagle compared with the value of the silver coinage. The new gross weight for the Quarter Eagle that was adopted to stop this practice was 64.5 grains, or 4.18 grams, and the purity of the metal was now 89.92 percent pure gold and 10.08 percent copper and silver. In January 1837, there was another minor adjustment, with the gold content increased to 90 percent.

1804 Crosslet-4 Eagle (Photo courtesy of Stack's)

A BRIEF LOOK AT OTHER DENOMINATIONS OF AMERICAN GOLD COINS

For a long time, it was thought that the only Dollar coins that were necessary were those made of silver, but in 1849, after the fabled gold strike in California, Dollar coins made of gold began being minted. This coin was designed to be used for two reasons. The first reason was the acute shortage of small silver coins in the late 1840s and early 1850s, and it was felt that a gold Dollar would alleviate some of the problem. The second reason, and more important politically, involved the declining gold deposits at the two Southern gold mints (Dahlonega and Charlotte); their elected representatives in Congress felt that gold supplies would stretch farther at these mints with the striking of gold Dollars. The gold Dollar was minted for forty years and was last made in 1889.

With the introduction of the gold Dollar, speculation arose about whether other denominations of gold coins would be useful in facilitating commerce. Pursuant to this, a gold Three Dollar coin was first

1849 Gold Dollar (Photo courtesy of Stack's)

issued in 1854, when 136,618 coins were minted — a huge amount by many standards. This coin turned out not to be very useful, and by the time of the Civil War, it was out of fashion, but it continued to be made until 1889.

The so-called Stella gold coin is actually a pattern $4 gold piece that was struck for only two years — 1879 and 1880. This is a very odd coin that was devised by Dr. William Wheeler Hubbell to destroy the age-old "rivalry" between gold and silver; the alloy was simply a variant of electrum, although Hubbell managed to persuade the U.S. Patent Office that it was something new. In addition, Hubbell was using the concept to promote metric coinage for use in world trade. The Stella was so named because of the large star on the reverse and the inscription "One Stella 400 cents." Some Stella pieces were struck in other metals, such as aluminum, for collectors.

Several varieties of the Stella were struck, and they had either the image of Liberty with long, flowing hair or the image of Liberty with coiled hair. The flowing hair pieces were designed by the Mint's chief

1881 Three Dollar Gold (Photo courtesy of Stack's)

engraver, Charles Barber, while the coiled hair variety was the work of George Morgan, Barber's assistant at the time. Morgan became chief engraver after Barber's death in 1917 and is most famous for the "Morgan Dollar."

Only 425 of the Flowing Hair Stella coins were struck dated 1879, and they were primarily sold, at cost, to members of the U.S. Congress. Many of these were turned into jewelry, which can absolutely destroy the value of a coin to a collector. There is a legend, probably apocryphal, that some of these exceedingly rare and valuable coins ended up around the necks of congressional mistresses, bordello madams, and call girls. (The 1879 Coiled Hair pieces as well as those dated 1880 were struck in small numbers for collectors.)

The last gold coin that needs to be discussed is the $20 gold piece, or the "Double Eagle," which was authorized by Congress the same time as the gold Dollar. This is the largest-denomination gold coin minted for circulation by the United States, and it first appeared in 1850 as a direct result of the discovery of gold in California. Not only

1879 Flowing Hair Stella, $4 Gold (Photo courtesy of Stack's)

did the gold strikes make available vast amounts of gold to be turned into coins, but they also brought to the forefront of the public's attention the notion of gold as a monetary device. In addition, the U.S. Treasury Department had not yet started printing paper currency, and a $20 gold piece was considered a necessity for bank reserves and international trade.

As discussed, minting for circulation of the Double Eagle began in 1850, but the first trial strikes (patterns) of 1849 consisted of just two coins in Proof state. Today these coins are extremely rare. One is in the Smithsonian Institution, and the other one was given to then Treasury Secretary William M. Meridith and later sold as part of his estate. The current whereabouts of the Meredith specimen is unknown.

These coins were 90 percent pure gold and 10 percent copper and contained just a little less than a full ounce of precious metal (.9675 troy ounce to be exact). At 34 millimeters in diameter, the new Double Eagle was a bit smaller than the silver Dollar. The first design of these coins was prepared by James B. Longacre and contained a portrait of

1861 Double Eagle (Photo courtesy of Stack's)

Liberty facing left surrounded by a circle of stars and the date on the obverse and a Heraldic Eagle on the reverse.

The familiar motto "In God We Trust" was added to this coin in 1866, and in 1877 the value stated on the coin went from "Twenty D." to "Twenty Dollars." The Longacre design was replaced by one created by Augustus Saint-Gaudens in 1907. President Teddy Roosevelt decided that the design of American coins lacked quality compared to European examples, and he prevailed on his friend Saint-Gaudens, who was arguably the most famous American sculptor of the day, to produce a new design for the Double Eagle.

The design that Saint-Gaudens proposed featured a resolute image of Liberty on the obverse striding among rays of light and carrying an olive branch. On the reverse, an eagle was depicted flying across the sun. Unfortunately, Saint-Gaudens saw the coin as a piece of sculpture, not as a coin to be manufactured and circulated. The coin was so ambitious and in such high relief that it required an elaborate series of strikes and heat treatments to produce it. The Mint complained, but Roosevelt

1881 Double Eagle (Photo courtesy of Stack's)

said he did not care if only one coin could be minted in a day — he wanted the redesign. Eventually, the Mint prevailed, and Charles Barber redesigned the coin so it could be manufactured in just one strike like the other coins the Mint made.

THE 1933 SAINT-GAUDENS DOUBLE EAGLE

The Saint-Gaudens Double Eagle continued to be made until 1933. In that year, 445,525 were minted between March 15 and May 19. But despite this rather large number, the government has claimed that no Double Eagle with this date was ever legally released for circulation.

A general banking crisis in the early 1930s occurred in the United States. The stock market crash of October 1929 had caused many financial institutions to close their doors, and in 1933 President Franklin D. Roosevelt issued Executive Order #6102, which was later incorporated into the Gold Reserve Act of 1934, outlawing the possession of gold coins by private individuals, except for those with value as collectibles,

1933 Double Eagle (Photo courtesy of U.S. Mint)

and declaring that these coins were no longer legal tender. The act required Americans to exchange any gold coins they might have for paper money, and, as a result, huge amounts of gold coins were melted down, including most of the 1933 Double Eagles.

In effect, F.D.R. removed the United States from the gold standard and made it illegal to convert paper money into gold, thus stopping runs on banks. He also placed an embargo on gold exports to protect the nation's supply of the precious metal. It remained illegal for U.S. citizens to own gold bullion until the end of 1974, when President Gerald Ford signed legislation that made ownership lawful once again.

But what about those 445,525 Double Eagles that were mainly being stored in the Mint's vaults? Well, 445,057 were melted down in 1934, but out of this number, 466 were sent out for testing and 29 were destroyed in the process. The remaining 437 coins were returned to the cashier's vault, where they remained until they, too, were melted down — reportedly, on February 6 and March 18, 1937. Two of the 1933 Double

Eagle coins, however, were sent to the Smithsonian, and these were supposedly the only two of these coins that survived.

Almost everyone believed that only two of these Double Eagles were extant, but what was not widely known until 1944 was that a number of these coins were in existence. In 1937, a Philadelphia jeweler sold a genuine 1933 Double Eagle to coin dealer James MacAllister. MacAllister then bought a total of five of these coins — three for $300 each and two for $350 each. These coins were quickly resold, and some of the finest coin collections in America soon included a 1933 Double Eagle.

The Philadelphia jeweler also sold four more coins to two other dealers, and these also soon found other homes. Then, in 1944, representatives of King Farouk of Egypt bought one of these coins from a Fort Worth, Texas, coin dealer, B. Max Mehl. Subsequently, Egyptian diplomats applied to the Treasury Department seeking permission to export the coin to Egypt under a provision of federal law that granted an exception for the exportation of rare coins.

Surprisingly, this apparently did not ring any alarm bells at the Treasury, which proceeded to send the coin to the Smithsonian, which vetted it as a rare coin of special interest to collectors. With this endorsement, the proper licenses were issued, and the coin was placed in the diplomatic pouch and sent on its way to Cairo.

All was well until Ernest Kehr of the *New York Herald Tribune* learned that a local auction house was about to sell a rare 1933 Double Eagle from a famous collection. Kehr rather innocently sent a letter to the Mint asking how many 1933 Double Eagles had been released to the public. Research at the Mint revealed that no 1933 Double Eagle had been issued for circulation — and, finally, the light went on, and the alarms were sounded.

The Secret Service was notified, and an aggressive investigation was instigated, revealing that a number of coins were in the possession of U.S. citizens, and by 1945, seven had been confiscated. The eighth coin was turned over after court action, and the ninth coin surfaced in 1952. All were melted down in an act that coin specialist David Akers called "a crime against numismatics."

At least one, however, was still in private hands, and that was the one that had been bought by Egypt's King Farouk, who was a collector of everything from Fabergé eggs to aspirin bottles and tins. There it resided until King Farouk was deposed in 1952, and many of his lavish possessions were scheduled for sale at a 1954 Cairo auction by Sotheby's, including the legendary 1933 Double Eagle coin.

It was listed as lot #185, but before the time of the sale, the United States asked for the return of the coin, and the Egyptian government agreed. The coin was withdrawn from the auction, but before it could be turned over to the United States, it inexplicably vanished.

Forty years passed, and then, in 1996, the Secret Service arrested Stephen Fenton at the Waldorf-Astoria Hotel in New York City and confiscated a 1933 Double Eagle. Fenton, an English coin dealer, initially told agents that he had bought the coin over the counter at his London coin shop, but he later changed his story to say that it was indeed the one that had once belonged to King Farouk.

The saga of the coin coming into Fenton's hands really begins with Andre de Clermont, another London coin dealer, who had established a buying relationship with an Egyptian jeweler. This jeweler had been acquiring rare coins from an Egyptian colonel, and the coins that de Clermont was purchasing matched the unsold coins found in the catalog of the 1954 Farouk sale.

Over time, the coins that the Egyptian jeweler was providing to de Clermont became rarer and more valuable, until de Clermont had to seek a partner to help with the financing of the deals. He chose Stephen Fenton. Finally, de Clermont asked about the fabled 1933 Double Eagle, and basically the jeweler said that he would make inquiries and see what could be done.

After much deliberation in Egypt, a packet of coins arrived in London in 1995 — and among them was the 1933 Double Eagle that theoretically had once belonged to King Farouk. Some say it was still in the Sotheby's envelope, and the entire grouping of coins — including the 1933 Double Eagle — was sold to de Clermont and Fenton for a reported $220,000. It was nothing less than a solid-gold bargain.

The partnership of Fenton and de Clermont started searching right away for someone to buy the 1933 Double Eagle, which brought the coin's existence to the attention of Jack Moore, who called the FBI, which passed Moore along to the Secret Service, who decided to try a sting operation to recover the elusive coin.

Moore and the English partnership negotiated, and a price of $1,500,000 was agreed upon, but Moore insisted that the 1933 Double Eagle had to be delivered to him in the United States, because he was not going to leave the country.

A meeting was set to take place in a hotel room in New York City's Waldorf-Astoria Hotel on February 8, 1996. As the transaction took place, Secret Service agents rushed into the room, confiscated the 1933 Double Eagle, and arrested Fenton.

In jail, Fenton was offered a public defender, but since he could pay for services, he contacted Barry Berke of Kramer Levin Naftalis & Frankel. Berke quickly got Fenton out on bond and soon after got his passport returned. By April 1996, Berke also was instrumental in getting the criminal charges against Fenton dismissed, but the coin itself was still in governmental hands, and the government intended to keep it there.

Berke, in a series of skillful arguments, asserted that the government had forfeited its claim to the coin in 1944, when it issued the export license to the representatives of King Farouk. In September 2000, the two sides began negotiating and came to an agreement just before the scheduled trial in late January 2001. Neither side cared to discuss the well-founded rumors of the existence of several more such coins.

In a decision reminiscent of Solomon, it was agreed that the government and Fenton would split the proceeds from a sale of the coin, which indeed did take place on July 20, 2002, in a New York auction conducted by the well-known numismatic firms of Sotheby's and Stack's. In a little over eight minutes, the 1933 Double Eagle was hammered down at $6.6 million, which came to $7.59 million after the 15 percent buyer's premium was added. After the sale was over, a brief ceremony was held in which the Mint formally placed the coin in circulation so the new owner could legally possess it.

The story took an unexpected, strange twist in 2004, when the family of the jeweler originally involved in the 1930s' selling of the 1933 Double Eagles found ten more of the pieces and turned them over to the U.S. Mint for authentication. The Mint announced in 2005 that it would not return them, and the matter has been tied up in the courts ever since.

The saga of the 1933 Double Eagle sounds like something out of the fevered imagination of a movie writer, but it is true. Also true is the story of the 1804 Plain-4 Eagle, which is actually much rarer than the 1933 Double Eagle and has a past that in many ways is more exciting and intriguing.

CHAPTER SIX

The Stage Is Set: Edmund Roberts's First Voyage

Although some early United States coins are Prooflike in appearance, the young mint did not produce these fine Proof coins until 1817. Since we are discussing the 1804 Plain-4 Proof Eagle, it is probably a good idea to define at this juncture what is meant by a Proof coin.

Many might suppose that the word "Proof" refers to the current condition of a coin, but it does not. Rather, it means a coin that has been minted in a special way. First, special "planchets," or coin blanks, are selected and polished, and then the dies that will be used to strike the Proof coin are highly polished.

During the striking process, the planchets are hand fed into the stamping machine. Each planchet is generally struck twice to increase the sharpness and detail of the images. Because both dies and planchets are highly polished before the coins are struck, the finished product has a brilliant, mirrorlike surface. The devices, such as the head of Liberty, generally have a "frosted" surface, but this is not always true.

Proof coins have always been prestige items made primarily for collectors, but when most modern collectors think of Proof sets, they consider 1936 as a starting point, even though full sets of Proof coins had been made available to collectors as early as the 1840s. The 1936 set consisted of a Cent, a Nickel, a Dime, a Quarter, and a Fifty-Cent piece. Today, U.S. Proof sets can be obtained with different configurations that might include five statehood Quarters, various commemorative coins, or presidential Dollars.

The Philadelphia Mint had the capability to make Proof coins but chose not to do so before 1817, probably because the chief coiner felt that the Prooflike specimens were adequate for visitors and collectors alike. Then, during the early morning hours of January 11, 1816, a fire at the Mint halted production of gold and silver coins for more than a year. The fire did not affect the main mint building, but it did damage a wooden outbuilding that housed the Mint's rolling mills.

These rolling mills were used to flatten gold and silver ingots to proper coin thickness, so planchets could be made that would later be used in the coin presses (housed in one of the main mint buildings) to manufacture the coins themselves. Before the fire, these rolling mills were not smooth enough to readily produce blanks that were uniform, with smooth, problem-free surfaces, so that Proof coins could be made with relative ease in the coin presses.

After the fire, Mint Director Robert Patterson saw an opportunity to upgrade the Mint's equipment and convinced the Treasury that the old mills were damaged beyond repair. Patterson ordered new ones from England that were built to his specifications, and they were installed in the Mint in the spring of 1817.

By the time the new rolling mills arrived, they could be housed in a new brick building that was not so susceptible to fire. The fire prompted other changes, and Patterson remodeled and repaired other parts of the Philadelphia Mint buildings over the weeks and months following the fire.

One of the most important improvements was the installation of a steam engine that was designed to drive the new rolling mills. Before this time, the mills's power had been provided by men and horses, thus the steam engine represented a big improvement in the efficiency of the new rolling mills. For almost twenty years, the steam engine ran the rolling mills, but the coin presses were still powered the old-fashioned way. A new Philadelphia Mint opened in 1833, and on March 23, 1836, steam-powered coining presses were introduced, nearly a year after the last 1804 Plain-4 Eagle was coined.

The use of steam power enabled mint workmen to produce better-quality planchets, and to do so more quickly and efficiently. However, steam power itself was not essential to the actual striking of Proof coins. In fact, non-steam-driven screw presses were used by the Mint for decades to make Proof coins, long after the mint began using steam-powered presses for regular coins.

Although Proof coins had been struck in sets for collectors as early as the 1840s, there was a hiatus in the early 1850s due to heavy coinage demands. Proof coinage resumed in a limited way in 1854, but the sale of complete sets was not formalized until 1858. For four decades prior to that, however, the Mint had produced limited quantities of Proof coins each year to satisfy a modest demand from the small but dedicated group of collectors that had access to the Philadelphia Mint.

Prior to 1860 these coins were provided at face value as a goodwill gesture to citizens interested in the Mint and its operations. Relatively few people took advantage of the service, partly because the number of numismatists was very small, and partly because, even at face value, the cost of the special coins (particularly the Proof gold coins) was significant by the standards of the day.

Before we discuss the actual birth of the 1804 Plain-4 Eagle, it is important to understand the background of the Mint in the early nineteenth century, when American gold was undervalued with respect to silver, and American gold coins were being shipped to Europe, where they were melted down for a profit and the metal used to mint European coins.

Mint Director Elias Boudinot

There was also a problem with silver Dollars in that many of them were shipped overseas — particularly to China — to purchase goods, and these coins stayed in China, never to return to the United States. These problems caused Mint Director Elias Boudinot to stop production in 1804 of both the $10 gold Eagle and the $1 silver coin.

In 1804, silver Dollars were officially minted, to the amount of 19,570 specimens, but these were struck with older dies, probably dated 1803. The small number of 3,757 Eagles dated 1804 was also struck for circulation that year, but these all had a Crosslet 4 in the date, and not the Plain 4, as does the coin under discussion here. We now know that at least fifteen 1804 silver Dollars are in existence, and there are only four 1804 Eagles with Plain 4's. But where did these coins come from? That is the question of the hour.

THE STORY BEGINS

In order to answer the questions about the origins of the 1804 silver Dollar and the 1804 Plain-4 Eagle, a brief examination of the life and times of Andrew Jackson needs to be undertaken. Suffice it to say that neither the 1804 silver Dollar nor the 1804 Plain-4 Eagle was minted in 1804 but instead was struck in 1834 and 1835 under the auspices of the U.S. State Department and President Andrew Jackson.

In the early 1830s, during Jackson's first term in the White House, the State Department became vitally interested in establishing trade relations with a number of Asiatic countries — some important and some not so important. This was one of the first stirrings of internationalism in the young United States, which understandably had been somewhat preoccupied with domestic issues during its formative years.

To lay the groundwork for possible future trade agreements, the State Department decided to send a special agent to visit some of these countries. These turned out to be Siam (modern Thailand), Muscat (modern Oman), Cochin China (modern Vietnam), and Japan. The idea was to open up trade discussions with the rulers of these countries, and Secretary of the Navy Levi Woodbury recommended New Hampshire native Edmund Roberts for the job.

Roberts had had some business reverses and was looking for a government appointment to help him through difficult financial times. In due course, he secured the diplomatic commission, and in 1832 he set sail aboard the naval sloop *U.S.S. Peacock* for destinations known only to him.

The original *Peacock* had been launched in 1813. It was 119 feet long and was rated to carry eighteen guns. It was built in New York City and dismantled there in 1828 in order to build a new *U.S.S. Peacock*. The new ship was a foot shorter than the old one but had the same 559-ton displacement of the original ship and the same gun complement. This new *Peacock* was in service until 1841, when it was lost on a sandbar in the Pacific Ocean off the coast of present day Washington State, near the mouth of the Columbia River. Roberts's mission or "embassy" was secret, and the captain of the *Peacock* was told by the Department of the Navy in a confidential letter that Roberts was to be received on the ship as a "Captain's Clerk" and would be expected to perform the duties of that position. However, the letter went on to say that Roberts was to be treated like a gentleman who enjoyed the confidence of the government, and that he had some sort of vague special assignment in "India, Arabia, and Africa."

The instructions given to Roberts by the State Department were much more specific. Roberts's letter of commission from Secretary of

The Early Life of Edmund Roberts

Edmund Roberts was born on June 29, 1785, to Edmund and Sarah Roberts of Portsmouth, New Hampshire. He was the couple's only son, but he had a sister, Sarah. Tragedy struck the family in 1787, when his father died.

Edmund's mother, Sarah, in 1789 married a Captain Moses Woodward, but he was not a caring stepfather. When their mother died in 1801, the two children essentially found themselves orphans.

Young Edmund went to Buenos Aires, Argentina, to live with his Uncle Josiah Joseph Roberts, who was in the shipping business, and subsequently traveled throughout South America, the West Indies, and England. Edmund purchased in 1806 his first ship, the *Robert*. That same year, he inherited his uncle's business and settled in Portsmouth.

In 1808, Roberts married Catherine Whipple Langdon, daughter of Judge Woodbury Langdon and niece of Governor John S. Langdon, and together they had eight children — six daughters and two sons. Their first son, Edmund Jr., died in infancy in 1820. A second Edmund Roberts Jr. was born in 1828, but he died during his second year. Catherine passed away on October 2, 1830.

From 1807 to 1823, Roberts operated almost a dozen ships in trade between the United States and the West Indies, as well as Europe. At least one of these ships, the *Mars*, is listed as a "privateer," which means it was a sort of governmentally authorized pirate that attacked "enemy" shipping (primarily during the War of 1812, when "privateering" was legal).

In 1807, Roberts's financial troubles started when the French seized his ship *Victory* in Cherbourg harbor. After the War of 1812, shipping in Portsmouth declined significantly, but instead of moving his fortune to other interests, Roberts doggedly stayed in the shipping business, and by around 1819, his fortune was quite depleted, if not gone.

Roberts began looking for a way to repair his fortunes. His attempted financial ventures in Zanzibar failed, costing him and his friends a significant amount of money. He tried for diplomatic posts and finally was appointed special envoy to Muscat, Cochin China, Japan, and Siam due to the support of his relative, Secretary of the Navy Levi Woodbury.

State Edward Livingston, dated January 27, 1832, gives more specific details about his clandestine mission:

> The President having named you his agent for the purpose of examining in the Indian Ocean, the means of extending the commerce of the United States by commercial arrangement with the powers whose dominions border on these seas, you will embark on board of the United States sloop of war, the *Peacock*, in which vessel (for the purpose of concealing your uniform from powers whose interest it might be to thwart the objects the President has in view) you will be rated as Captain's Clerk. Your real character is known to Captain Geisinger, and needs not to be to any other person on board, unless you find it necessary for the purpose of your mission to communicate it to others.
>
> As you will enter the Indian Ocean from the eastward, the first place at which your duties will begin will be Cochin China. Here you will proceed to the capital of the country Hue, sometimes called Huefoo, or such other of the royal cities as the king may reside at. You will, in your passage to this place, inform yourself minutely of the trade carried on between the kingdom and the kingdom and the countries — the nature of the products of the country, whether natural, agricultural, or manufactured — the maritime and military strength, and of the articles of merchandise of personal consumption or demanded for their own commerce with other nations of the favors granted to or exactions made upon the commerce of the various nations who trade with them.
>
> On your arrival you will present yourself to the king with your power and the letter addressed to him. You will state that the President having heard of his fame for justice and desire to improve the advantages of commerce for the good of his people has sent you to inquire whether he is willing to admit our ships into his harbors with such articles of merchandise as will be useful to him and his people, and to receive in return the products of their industry or of their soil. That we manufacture and can bring arms, ammunitions, cloths of cotton and wool, glass, &c (enumerating all the articles that you find they usually import), that we can furnish them cheaper than any other nation because it is against the principles of our nation to build forts or make expensive establishments in foreign countries, that we never make conquests, or ask any nation to let us establish

> ourselves in their countries as the English, the French, and the Dutch have done in the East Indies.
>
> All we ask is free liberty to come and go for the purpose of buying and selling, paying obedience to the laws of the country while we are there. But that while we ask no exclusive favor, we will not carry our commerce where we are treated worse than other nations. We will pay all the duties that are required by the King's authority, but we will not submit to pay more than any other nation does, nor will we bear the exactions of any of his subordinate officers, that the President is very powerful, has many ships of war at his command, but that they are only used to protect our commerce against imposition, that the King wishes to secure the advantages of our trade, he may enter into a treaty by which the above stipulations must be secured to our merchants, that as soon as it is known, our ships will resort to his ports, enriching him by the duties that he will receive, and his subjects by their commerce.
>
> An important point is to obtain an explicit permission to trade, generally, with the inhabitants, for it is understood that at most, or all of the ports, the Mandarins or other officers, now monopolize the commerce, permitting none of the inhabitants to trade with foreigners.
>
> You will be furnished with a power to conclude a treaty if one can be obtained on the terms above specified and such others shall hereafter be mentioned, and to promise, which you may do verbally or in writing, *that the usual presents shall be made on the exchange of the ratification of which you may settle a list of such things as may be most agreeable, not exceeding ten thousand dollars in value for each power.*
>
> Your compensation will be six dollars per diem, and all necessary personal expenses, which last can only be in unforeseen cases, as your subsistence on board the ship is provided for. An advance will be made to you of one thousand dollars on account of your pay and two hundred dollars for such presents as may be necessary to gain an audience.
>
> The above instructions will govern you in your missions to Siam and the powers of Arabia on the Red Sea where you will also be conveyed. . . . (Bowers 1999, 143)

The *Peacock* sailed on March 8, 1832. It was supposed to be accompanied by an escort vessel, the *U.S.S. Boxer*, which was a smaller ship that could get closer into coastal waters than could the larger *Pea-*

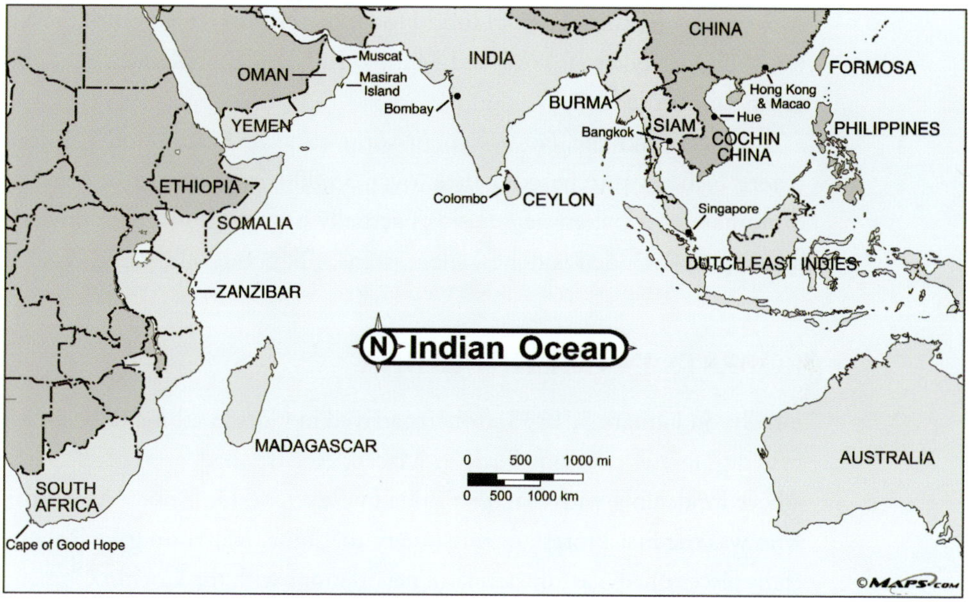

Indian Ocean Map (Photo courtesy of Maps.com)

cock. However, by the time the *Peacock* had reached Buenos Aires, the *Boxer* was still not on the scene. The *Peacock* sailed south toward South America and made its first stop at the Cape Verde Islands (Porto Prayo, near St. Jago). On May 3, the ship reached Rio de Janeiro.

While still in South America, the itinerary of the *Peacock* was changed. Instead of sailing west around Cape Horn at the tip of South America, the ship would sail east and go around the Cape of Good Hope at the tip of the African continent. This meant that instead of visiting Cochin China first, it was envisioned that Roberts would initially visit Muscat although the original plan was followed after all.

Exactly where Roberts was going on his trade treaty mission was still somewhat up in the air, with written discussions about visits to Burma, Sumatra (the King of Acheen), and Japan being proposed.

After rounding the Cape of Good Hope, the *Peacock* sailed on to Sumatra, then to Krakatoa, Java, and Manila. In Manila, cholera struck, and seven sailors died.

Roberts and the *Peacock* spent some time in Macao and Canton, where Roberts purchased a little over $3,000 in goods to be used as diplomatic gifts when negotiations actually began with foreign powers. These gifts included watches, silver items, silk goods, and delicacies.

ROBERTS IN COCHIN CHINA

Finally, on January 5, 1833, Roberts arrived in Cochin China to begin his first diplomatic mission. Back in Macao, Roberts had been given some advice for dealing with Cochin China by Reverend Dr. Robert Morrison, who was the first Protestant missionary to China. Morrison gave Roberts eight pieces of advice for successful negotiations with the Cochin Chinese:

1. Always tell the strict truth. Morrison said to give as the reason for coming, "We come to China for refreshment and refreshment we must have. We come to Cochin China to speak on national affairs, and an audience we must have."
2. Resist the terms that an interview with the king or emperor usually entails, namely, uncovering the feet and knocking one's head on the ground (called "kowtowing").
3. Negotiations must not be based on a lord and vassal relationship but on mutual reciprocity.
4. Never depend on the advice of "friendly natives." Use your own judgment of what is right and appropriate.
5. Do not make yourself too cheap; be kind and courteous to all, but after some little formalities.
6. Take your ships as near the capital as practical, and tell inferior officials as little as possible.
7. Do not expect to get concessions from unreasonable demands or insults.
8. A little pageantry in clothing will impress the uncivilized mind.

— Roberts papers, New Hampshire Historical Society
(Bowers 1999, 163)

Of course, the Reverend Dr. Morrison's view of the Cochin Chinese being "uncivilized" was reflected in the Cochin Chinese views that Europeans and Americans were barbarians — at the very best. The negotiations from the *Peacock* were somewhat handicapped, because the ship had not anchored where it was supposed to. Due to adverse winds, it had not been able to go into the harbor in the Bay of Turon (a violation of Morrison's rule #6) and so had to settle for Vung-lam, a minor harbor town on Phuyen Bay, about fifty miles outside of Hue.

Negotiations with local officials produced no results, but on January 8, a Roman Catholic priest arrived who did not even know where North America was, much less anything at all about the United States. This turned into something of a farce, but soon a representative from the Cochin Chinese Ministry of Commerce and Navigation arrived — however, at this point, things actually went from bad to worse.

It was stated that if Roberts were allowed to meet the Cochin Chinese king (emperor) that Roberts would have to kowtow (a violation of Morrison's rule #2), and that he (Roberts) would also have to exhibit an attitude of "silent awe" while in the emperor's presence. This meant that Roberts would have had to keep his hands uplifted at all times during the audience. This did not bode well for Roberts's mission.

The situation continued to deteriorate. Local merchants charged exorbitant prices for water and supplies, and they gave misleading answers as to how one might actually get to Hue — including the thin excuse that local officials actually did not remember how to get there — and if they eventually managed to remember, the route was difficult and dangerous.

On January 17, a deputation from Hue arrived, and it might be imagined that serious negotiations to begin talks with the Cochin Chinese would begin — but they did not. An exasperating game of cat and mouse ensued, with nothing being gained by either side. Then, on January 26, a gift arrived from the Cochin Chinese king/emperor. It was a sumptuous meal consisting of fifty-one dishes, containing everything from duck to dog — but the Americans refused to eat it and picked at only one of the dishes (a confection).

The Americans were appalled by the local standards of cleanliness and envisioned the food being prepared using dirty pots by cooks with unwashed hands employing food contaminated with vermin. Roberts soon learned that the king of Cochin China had not been informed of their mission, and that he and his men had been involved in some sort of Asian diplomatic charade. Frustrated, Roberts and the *Peacock* left Cochin China with nothing accomplished and sailed for their next stop, which was Siam.

SUCCESS IN SIAM

Things went well in Siam from the very beginning. In a matter of days, Roberts and his men had been greeted by the Ph'ra Klang, or the Siamese diplomatic minister, who organized entertainment for the Americans and saw to it that they were fed well. It was made clear to Roberts that the Ph'ra Klang needed to be the recipient of important gifts, so Roberts gave him a gold and pearl watch, two cases of silks, and four filigreed silver baskets edged with gold and decorated with enameled figures. This, however, turned out to be not quite enough.

Roberts had to sweeten the gift with 100 silver Dollars — the first of Roberts's diplomatic gift of coins. This seemed to work, and within a few days, Roberts was on his way to see His Magnificent Majesty, King Ph'ra Nang Klao, also known as Rama III. Once again, the problem of the kowtow raised its proverbial ugly head. Roberts was told that he would be required to go through this humiliating ceremony, but he refused, saying it was not the custom of his country to show servility to rulers of foreign governments.

Roberts and his fellow Americans were excused from performing this ritual — to a point. Roberts and his men were required to perform a modified version of the ritual and, upon sitting down, they were required to place their feet behind them and make three bows that involved placing the palms of their hand together and touching them to their foreheads and then their chests (breasts). They were not required to remove their shoes, as was the custom.

At the appointed hour, the Roberts party was led into the reception rooms at the Hall of Justice, and they were not impressed with what they saw. They later commented about the tackiness of the decoration on the room's columns and were derisive of the carpet, which they said could be purchased in the United States for about $1.25 a square yard.

Roberts walked into the room and found himself being presented to a man whom he described as being a "very stout and fleshy man," seated on a low throne and dressed in short pants with a tissue of gold cloth around his shoulders. The man was surrounded by as many as 400 men, all face down on the ground in full kowtow, but Roberts walked up with his shoes on (something that most diplomats were not allowed to do) and merely bowed in respect to the king.

Just Who Was King Ph'ra Nang Klao?

Is this the Siamese king Westerners know so well from the movie and stage play *The King and I*? The answer is no, but there is still an interesting story here.

The royal line that still rules Thailand was founded by Buddha Yodfa Chulalongkom, who reigned from 1782 to 1809. Some refer to him as Rama I, but that is not entirely correct. He was succeeded in 1809 by Buddha Loetla Nabalai, who ruled until 1824 and is incorrectly referred to as "Rama II."

This king had approximately thirty-eight wives, and Crown Prince Mongkut was supposed to succeed him. Mongkut had seventy-two brothers and sisters, but his title to the throne was indisputable. However, he had a half brother, Nang Klao, or Prince Chesda Bondindra, who was more experienced in government. When the old king died in 1824, he was succeeded by Nang Klao, while Mongkut became a Buddhist monk. It was Nang Klao whom Edmund Roberts dealt with in the 1830s.

When Nang Klao died in 1851, he had no queen and, therefore, no child who could inherit the throne of Siam. Mongkut came to the throne and became the only king who chose to be called "Rama" — in this case, "Rama IV" — because he chose to adopt the English style of numbering its kings and queens. It was Mongkut who hired Anna Leonowens of *Anna and the King of Siam* and *The King and I* fame, but more about that a little later.

Roberts subsequently sat on the carpet in the manner discussed above, and small talk ensued about the health of President Andrew Jackson and other great men in the United States, and about the other places the *Peacock* had visited on its voyage.

At the end, the king asked Roberts to submit a written list to the Ph'ra Klang containing all of the things the American mission wanted from Siam. The audience took about thirty minutes, and when it was over, a curtain was pulled in front of the king, and the American group left the hall.

After the audience, Roberts tried to send the king some of the diplomatic gifts that had been purchased in China, but the king refused them, saying that he had — or could get — all the Chinese items he wanted. What he wanted was to be given things from the United States, particularly luxury goods that were not readily available to him in Siam. This position would have great bearing on the 1804 Plain-4 gold Eagle, which would be struck at the mint after Roberts returned to the United States.

With many Asian rulers, this refusal of gifts might have signaled an end to trade negotiations, but in this case it did not. Over the next two weeks, an agreement was hammered out and translated into four languages — English, Siamese, Chinese, and Portuguese.

These various translations proved to be something of a problem in the future, because there were numerous translation mistakes, and some of the provisions in some of the versions were not consistent with one another. What did the United States get with this treaty? Perhaps the most important thing was status of "Most Favored Nation" when it came to trading, which meant a reduction of tariffs.

The treaty also stipulated that American citizens in Siam could not be imprisoned for discharge of their debts. Very interestingly, the Americans wanted a provision that would list opium as a commodity that could be traded to the Siamese. Very wisely, the Siamese disallowed this proviso.

According to the *Singapore Chronicle* of June 6, 1833, Roberts wanted the king and his trade minister to sign the treaty in duplicate so a copy could be forwarded to the United States immediately. It is reported that Roberts actually had three copies drawn up, but he could only get one signed because the trade minister was fearful that the other two might be used for some nefarious purpose that might damage his country's interests. In the end, despite many attempts at persuasion, Roberts was only able to get one copy of the treaty signed.

Once again, the problem of diplomatic gifts surfaced. The king sent suggestions of things he wanted to be given, reading like a "Dear Santa" list. The king's "wish list" included two mirrors with carved gilt frames that could be used as a screen and a back that was painted green. He also requested botanical specimens, flower pots, and "hairy" carpeting — whatever that might be.

Officials told Roberts that, in addition, the king wanted five pairs of statues in human form — life size or larger — that were clothed in the costumes of the United States. The king also desired numerous pairs of large, clear glass lamps and a pair of swords with slightly curved blades and hilts and scabbards made of solid gold, not gilt metal. These were items that Roberts was supposed to bring back when he returned with the ratified trade treaty.

The king sent Roberts some gifts, but these were extremely disappointing to Roberts, if not a bit insulting. Roberts did not understand that these were rare and treasured items taken from the Siamese rain forest, and he was very dismissive of their value. The gifts consisted of items such as elephant "teeth" (presumably ivory tusks), sugar, candy, pepper, tinware, and items that were used to make red and violet dyes and could be used as medicine.

Later, when the State Department asked Roberts to account for these gifts, he sent a rather huffy reply that they were of such little value that he left most of them behind in Asia. He claimed that some of the gifts were stolen, while others were sold in Canton for the paltry sum of $34.25. He also noted that some of the king's presents were eaten.

Roberts concluded that Siamese officials had confiscated and sold the real gifts sent by the king and substituted much lesser items in their stead. Despite these bumps in the road, the treaty was signed, and it became the first treaty between the United States and an Asian nation.

It is often referred to as the "Roberts Treaty," or the "Treaty of Amity and Commerce of 1833."

ON TO OMAN

The *Peacock* left Siamese waters on April 4, 1833, and the next scheduled stop was Singapore. The stop was short and uneventful, and the *Peacock* then sailed on to Jakarta (then called "Batavia"), Indonesia, and it was there that the ship was joined by the *U.S.S. Boxer*, its erstwhile escort and transporter of previously much-needed diplomatic gifts.

Roberts had been thinking of retracing his steps and paying a call on Japan, but he felt like he might need some very special diplomatic gifts to help make that journey successful. At Jakarta, Roberts took stock of the gifts the *Boxer* carried and decided that they were not nearly good enough to impress the august emperor of Japan.

It is impossible not to speculate what might have happened had Roberts decided to go to Japan two decades before Commodore Matthew Perry. World history might have been changed, and lucrative Japanese trade might have been opened to the United States, causing some changes in the balance of international economic power. But Roberts decided not to go to Japan and shipped the long-awaited diplomatic presents back to the United States. He stayed for some time in Jakarta, but on July 22, both the *Peacock* and the *Boxer* set sail, with Oman as their ultimate destination. Roberts had high hopes for concluding a treaty with Oman's sultan of Muscat, mainly because the sultan and Roberts had met some years before on Zanzibar, an archipelago located in the Indian Ocean off the east coast of Africa.

Roberts first met the sultan in 1828 while he (Roberts) was trying to recoup some of his family fortune by trading goods in Zanzibar. Zanzibar had come under the rule of the sultan of Muscat in 1698, and it was a place where the current Sultan, Seyyid Said-bin-Sultan, chose to reside, as the place was so much more pleasant than his native Oman. At the time, the sultan had actually made Zanzibar the capital of his empire.

It should be understood that Oman was an important power in the region, and that the sultan had the largest navy in the Indian Ocean, including that of the British. He had commercial and territorial interests up and down the East African coast. The territory under the control of the sultan of Muscat included not only Oman and Zanzibar but also much of the coast of present-day Iran and Baluchistan, which borders Iran, Afghanistan, and Pakistan.

In an earlier meeting, Roberts had sailed to Zanzibar on the *Mary Ann*. His voyage had been underwritten by friends back in the United States, and he had high hopes for the success of his trading venture. But upon his arrival in Zanzibar on October 8, 1827, those high hopes were soon dashed.

Basically, it was Roberts's intention to trade cargos, that is, to sell the goods he brought over from the New World and then to use the money to reload the ship with goods bought in Zanzibar. He expected to make large sums of money on both ends of this deal, but tariffs, plus anchorage and other fees, tended to eat up any profit that he might have made.

A Brief Biography of the Sultan of Muscat

Reportedly born in 1791 in Semail, Oman, the sultan of Muscat was the son of Seyyid Sultan-bin-Ahmed (or Said-bin-Sultan). His father was killed in battle on November 20, 1804, and was survived by seven sons and three daughters. In a rather odd twist of fate, the nominal heir to the throne, Prince Salem, did not have much interest in ruling and thus relinquished his rights to Seyyid Said-bin-Sultan, who was only thirteen at the time.

Because of his youth, a cousin, Seyyid Bedr, acted as regent, but the real authority seems to have resided with an aunt called "Binti Iman." An arrangement such as this was not destined to last, and Binti Iman told her nephew that his cousin was planning to murder him and take the throne for himself. With family approval, Seyyid Said-bin-Sultan had Seyyid Bedr killed and thus secured his right to rule.

By 1806, Seyyid Said-bin-Sultan was fully in charge of Oman, and he began a program of territorial expansion and dealing with warring tribes, which threatened his authority. He made Zanzibar the actual capital of his empire, and over time he gained a reputation for being an enlightened and a fair ruler (if one did not happen to be a slave).

In September 1856, on a trip from Muscat to Zanzibar, aboard his ship *Kitorie*, Sultan Seyyid Said-bin-Sultan developed pain at the site of an old wound in his thigh. Besides suffering from the infected wound, he also developed dysentery. He died at sea in the Indian Ocean on October 19, 1856.

Roberts fully expected the sultan's agents to give him a generous sum for his New World cargo and to allow him access to storage depots from which he could purchase goods for the return journey. He wanted ivory or gum copal (a resin used as a chemical base for incense, enamel, glue, varnish, paint, etc.) but soon found that these easily saleable commodities were not available — at least not to him.

He was a stranger in a strange land, and he had no connections with locals who could smooth the way for advantageous business transactions. He ended up selling much of his cargo for a loss and being offered cargo such as hides and dates. The hides were "stinking," and the price of the dates exceeded the retail price paid for dates in the local bazaar.

Fortunately, fate intervened in the form of a Frenchman who sent a letter under his own name to the sultan to whom Roberts had written. In the letter, the Frenchman (whose exact name is unknown) tells the sultan that his agents have treated the American (Roberts) very badly. The suggestion was made that if the sultan wanted to establish trade relations with the United States, then he needed to meet Roberts and perhaps ameliorate his situation.

The sultan had heard of the United States as a result of the War of 1812 and is said to have admired Americans for their enterprise. On January 27, 1828, Roberts wrote to the sultan, and subsequently a meeting was arranged. The two became friends, and the sultan suggested that a treaty might be arranged between his country and the United States. Roberts put forth the idea that trade with the United States might be more comfortable than trade with the British, because the Americans had no territorial interest in the region and were not in competition with Oman for influence over the people of the region.

Ultimately, the sultan did help Roberts in his trading mission, but it was too little too late. The disaster that had happened before the meetings with the sultan could not be completely undone. Roberts took on a cargo of medium- to low-gum copal — the higher grades of this substance come from younger trees, while the lower grades come from older trees.

Roberts also took on a cargo of dried dates, and upon returning to New York, the goods were sold off over a year's time. The result was a significant loss for the voyage, but it would have been much larger if the sultan had not intervened on his behalf.

MUSCAT LOVE

When the two warships (the *Peacock* and the *Boxer*) approached Muscat, a boat was dispatched to inform the sultan of Roberts's arrival. The response was very gratifying, because the sultan sent messages that he was very pleased to have the American vessels in his waters and glad about their mission. With the warm messages of welcome came quantities of fresh food, including grapes, dates, goats, and sheep.

Upon anchoring in the cove of Muscat, Roberts found the city to be less than inviting. He reported that there was nothing green to be seen — no trees, no shrubs, and not even a blade of grass. The cove itself was surrounded with jagged cliffs that soared 300 or 400 feet into the air and were crowned with circular towers that had once been part of the Portuguese stronghold. It was a desolate place (no wonder the sultan preferred to reside in Zanzibar).

Entering the town, Roberts saw two castles, the sultan's palace (not a very impressive place), and a few other stone houses. Roberts wrote that the larger buildings in the town of Muscat were "small, dark, and filthy, made of palm branches only, or at best covered with mats, or coated with mud, so that the periodical rains frequently demolish a considerable portion of the city, and they are seen floating in fragments through the streets, which are converted into so many canals, by the torrents of water which descend from the circumjacent mountains" (Bowers 1999, 174).

He went on to speak of people sleeping out in the open on mats laid on dirt, and about how they had one earthenware pot for cooking, which they accomplished by using camel dung or palm fronds for fuel. Roberts observed beggars everywhere and noted that the corners of the extremely narrow streets were filled with blind people who cried out to passersby for help in their plight.

Roberts played the tourist, making observations about everything from the sultan's horses to the slave market. He wrote of the women in veils and seemed to be nonplussed that they stared at him as he passed by, rather than turning their faces to the wall, as good Muslim women were supposed to do. He mentioned the Hindu barbers plying their trade in the streets, cutting hair, perfuming beards, and cutting toenails for all to see.

The day after their arrival, Roberts and his party met with the sultan. He was seeking, like in Siam, "Most Favored Nation" status, which involved the lowering of duties and port charges. When Roberts and the other men from the *Peacock* and the *Boxer* came into the sultan's presence, Roberts was pleased to note that there was no kowtowing or any other demeaning ritual to be observed, but that the sultan left his seat and came to meet them.

The talks with the sultan went very well and very quickly. The sultan agreed to "Most Favored Nation" status and set the import fee at 5 percent, with no other fees for pilotage, anchorage, and so forth being charged. Previously, American ships paid a 7.5 percent duty on imports and the same for exports, plus fees for anchorage and pilotage.

In other words, Roberts got a very good deal for American commercial interests in the region, and he did so quite easily. In effect, this also opened up most of the Indian Ocean ports in East Africa as well as in the Persian Gulf. It took about two weeks to finalize the treaty, and it was signed on September 21, 1833.

Once again, gifts were exchanged, and the sultan received three silver-filigreed enameled baskets (Chinese made), a box containing broadcloth, cashmere, and velvet (from the *Boxer* supply of diplomatic gifts), sweetmeats from Canton, two cases of Suchau pongee (pongee is a thin, soft fabric woven from raw silk), boxes of imperial tea, and a gold and enamel watch set with pearls. Roberts would bring back more impressive presents when he returned the ratified treaty, including one of the 1804 Plain-4 Eagles.

The *Peacock* and the *Boxer* sailed from Muscat on October 8, 1833, and they carried a letter from the sultan to Andrew Jackson, whom the sultan referred to as "the most high and mighty." The missive fairly gushed with goodwill toward the United States and closed with the notation that the letter was from Jackson's "most beloved friend."

Roberts left the *Peacock* in Rio de Janeiro and spent six weeks on shore before boarding the *U.S.S. Lexington* for the rest of the return trip to the United States. The ship sailed on March 1, 1834, and found itself off of Cape Cod on April 24. It anchored in Boston harbor on the 25th, which means that Roberts had been away from home for approximately twenty-six months.

After his return, Roberts conferred with President Andrew Jackson and the secretary of state, and all seemed to be going in his favor. The two treaties were ratified by the Senate on June 30, 1834, but the next day (July 1, 1834) Roberts's future as a diplomat became uncertain when a new secretary of state, John Forsyth, took office and immediately called into question Roberts's continued role as a diplomat.

W
S

CHAPTER SEVEN

A Great Rarity's Little-Noticed Birth

Despite the cloud hanging over Roberts's future in returning the treaties to Siam and Muscat, the question of making or acquiring diplomatic gifts fit for a king or Oriental potentate was moving forward. As mentioned earlier, the king of Siam wanted a pair of swords with scabbards made of solid gold, gilded metal. Contemporary newspaper reports indicate that these swords were a reality, and that they were fit for use by Richard the Lionhearted (King Richard I of England) or Saladin (Salah ad-Din, legendary sultan of Egypt and Syria).

Reportedly, the swords had blades of Damascus steel emblazoned with Asian symbols, and the scabbard was indeed pure gold. The maker was Marquand and Company, which had been founded circa 1815 as Marquand and Brother — the brothers referred to were Isaac (1766–1838) and Frederick Marquand (1799–1882). The firm became Marquand and Company in 1834 and was made up of Frederick and Josiah P. Marquand, as well as Erastus O. Thompkins. At the time these swords were crafted, Frederick Marquand was apparently the company's principal partner.

Roberts continued to pursue his idea of making a second voyage to return the ratified treaties and to take diplomatic gifts, and it finally found favor with the Jackson administration. There was much excitement to return to Siam and Muscat, but there was also a strong feeling that new overtures should be made to Cochin China and Japan.

The Siamese "wish list" was examined, and it was thought that procurement of the statues clothed in American dress would not be practical, but that the plants the king had requested were not a problem, other than a consideration of how grand their containers should be. As for the carpet specifically requested by the Siamese king, Roberts was instructed to shop around Boston and find something he thought might be suitable and most appreciated in Siam that might fit the description. He was then to send a carpet sample to New York so the purchase could be made.

There was some discussion about the proper gifts to be given to the sultan of Muscat, who had not supplied Roberts with a wish list. Roberts recommended a variety of items as being appropriate, including clocks, firearms, maps, model ships, and cut glass. One of the most interesting items ordered to be made for presentation was a steam engine mounted on a rail car that came with a 12-foot diameter track. This latter item was not ready by the time Roberts sailed for the Orient.

Perhaps the most intriguing and historically important gift of all was to be "a complete set of new gold & silver & copper coins of the United States neatly arranged in a morocco case" (Bowers 1999, 195). Secretary of State John Forsyth followed through with Roberts's suggestion and obtained approval for the coin set from President Jackson. In a letter to Mint Director Samuel Moore, dated November 11, 1834, Forsyth wrote, in part, as follows:

> The President has directed that a complete set of coins of the United States be sent to the King of Siam, and another to the Sultan of Muscat. You are requested, therefore, to forward to the Department for that purpose, duplicate specimens of each kind now in use, whether of gold, silver, or copper. (Newman and Bressett, 63)

In response, Moore decided to prepare Proof versions of the coins, meaning coins made with carefully polished dies struck on specially made planchets, to be included in the sets. These had to be specially made, but the Mint did not have current dies for two of the coins necessary to complete the set — the gold Eagle and the silver Dollar. Records showed that neither of these coins had been struck since 1804. This posed a dilemma for Director Moore, because although these two coins had not been struck for three decades, both types were still considered "now in use."

Mint Director Samuel Moore

Indeed, as the largest gold and silver coins, they would be the most likely to impress their intended recipients, and their absence would detract from their impact and appearance. Moore compromised — he would include these two coins in the sets but would use newly made dies that were dated 1804, the last year in which they were made, rather than 1834, which was the date shown on the other nine

Note that the two 1804 Plain-4 Proof Eagles were billed at a value of $10 each, but that was incorrect, because their gold composition of 270 grains, which was the correct weight for an 1804 Eagle, was slightly higher than the gold composition of the new Eagles produced once again beginning in 1838. The gold content for Eagles had been lowered by law in 1834, making the two antedated 1804 pieces slightly heavier and worth $10.66 instead of $10.

1804 Silver Dollar (Photo courtesy of Heritage Auctions, HA.com)

coins, including the copper Half Cent and large Cent; silver Half Dime, Dime, Quarter Dollar, and Half Dollar; gold Quarter Eagle with motto "E Pluribus Unum," another gold Quarter Eagle without the motto, and the Half Eagle.

Perhaps it should be noted that there were also two different Half Eagles made in 1834, but unlike the two examples of the Quarter Eagle, only one of the Half Eagles was included in the sets. Why the second version of the Half Eagle was left out while both Quarter Eagles were included in the diplomatic sets is open for speculation and conjecture.

Moore's decision to produce the two new dies for the 1804 silver Dollar and the 1804 gold Eagle led to the creation of two great numismatic treasures. The 1804 silver Dollar drew collectors' attention more quickly than did the 1804 Eagle Plain-4, because it was the only silver Dollar coin available with that date.

Although the Mint records show that 19,570 silver Dollars were minted in 1804, it is now known that all of them carried an earlier date, probably 1803. Presumably, this happened because the older dies were still useable in 1804, and it was the Mint's policy at the time to use dies until they wore out (making new ones was very expensive), regardless of exactly when the coins were actually struck from them. What this means in simplest terms is that before the Mint made some in 1834, there were no silver Dollars dated 1804 in existence.

Crosslet 4 (Photo courtesy of Stack's)

Plain 4 (Photo courtesy of Stack's)

As for the Eagles, 3,757 of these had been minted in 1804 with that date. The form of one of the numbers used in the date, however, was distinctive, in that the numeral 4 had a perpendicular line at the end of the crossbar. This configuration is called a "Crosslet-4," and it is ever so slightly different from the numeral 4 used on the dies made for the 1804 coin in 1834. That 1834 numeral 4 did not have the perpendicular line at the end of the crossbar, which led to this design being referred to as a "Plain-4." It is a tiny, tiny difference, but because it quickly distinguishes the early from the later production, it makes all the difference in the world — both as a means of identification and as a detail signifying to collectors its great rarity.

According to Eric Newman of the Numismatic Education Society, another difference between the 1804 Crosslet-4 and the rarer and more valuable 1804 Plain-4 is that there are 200 reeds around the edge of the 1804 Plain-4 but only 126 reeds around the edge of the Crosslet-4 examples. This distinction requires a great deal of patience and a sharp pair of eyes to determine, but it is a detail worth ascertaining.

The two types of 1804 Eagles are also distinguished by the fact that the original minting was a "business strike," meaning the coins were made without using carefully polished dies or special planchets. It should be noted that the U.S. Mint did not make Proof coins until 1817, so when Samuel Moore decided to make Proof coins for the diplomatic sets in 1834, he made great rarities of both the 1804 silver Dollar and the 1804 Eagle. Actually, the Mint did have the capability of making Proof coins prior to 1817 but apparently chose not to because of the relatively large amount of time involved.

Production of these coin sets did not happen overnight, but it did take place relatively quickly by the standards of the day. Examples of the two antedated coins, plus other Proof coins in the sets that were legitimately dated 1834, were ready by December 18, 1834. The special morocco-covered cases in which they were to be displayed were also ready. The one destined for the king of Siam was a saffron-yellow morocco, while the one intended for the sultan of Muscat was a burgundy hue.

THE CASE OF THE CASES

Secretary of State John Forsyth took very seriously the preparation of the presentation cases. In a letter dated December 2, 1834, to Samuel Moore, director of the Mint, he wrote:

> As the object of the Department in procuring the boxes for the coins which are intended to be sent as presents to Siam and Muscat is not only to preserve them from being soiled, but to show them to the greatest advantage, the color of the interior lining and the form of construction are left to your discretion. It is also thought best upon reflection, that the whole of the work, which is desired to be done upon the caskets should be executed at Philadelphia. After they have been prepared, therefore, in the way directed by a former letter from the Department, you will please to have them decorated on the exterior with some suitable device in gilding displaying the national emblems, the Eagle, stars &c., in such manner as

> may be agreeable to your own taste, or that of the artist employed. For the additional expense thus incurred, which it is presumed will not be considerable, you will be at liberty also to draw on the Department [of State]. If the articles are received here by the 20th of December, they will be in time to answer the purpose for which they are designed. (Bowers 1999, 195)

Moore took the task in hand with energy and, according to R. W. Julian in the January 1970 issue of *The Numismatist*:

> The Director [Moore] promptly retained Henry Havermill to prepare the special boxes for the coins. They turned out to be a very expensive item indeed. Havermill charged Moore $31.00 for his work in making the two cases; this artist must have spared neither labor nor expense and at this price they were truly fit for a king. Despite this cost they remained unfinished and were sent to Benjamin Garhill, also of Philadelphia, for the final touches. A special die was prepared and our national coat of arms was embossed on the cases. Garhill's statement of account amounted to $20, making a total of $51 on just the cases alone.

Initially, the Mint provided just two sets of these coins, but in the three months between the making of the sets and Roberts's proposed sailing date of April 10, 1835, it was decided that two more sets needed to be made. One was for the ruler of Cochin China and the other was for Japan.

It is presumed that these two additional sets had coins dated 1835, plus the silver Dollar and the Eagle dated 1804, but neither set was ever delivered to its intended recipient, and no one knows for sure about the 1835 dates. In any event, Roberts was to sail once again on the *Peacock*, and the Mint rushed the two new sets to be on board in time for the projected April sailing. (Roberts received the two additional sets on the 21st.)

It is reported that the government paid $12.75 in postage to get the sets to New York in time. That may seem like a piddling amount today, but at the time it was one week's wages for most working Americans. However, the *Peacock*'s departure was delayed until April 23, 1835.

The Second Philadelphia Mint, 1833–1901

Before continuing the story of the odyssey of Edmund Roberts and the 1804 Plain-4 Eagle, it is important to explain that when the Mint made the diplomatic set, it apparently made the four 1804 silver Dollars for the sets and then made four other examples, for a total of eight existing coins. However, it did not make any extra 1804 Plain-4 Eagles.

It is speculated that the Mint made the extra 1804 silver Dollars because these were the only specimens with that date — and they were also relatively inexpensive to produce. The fact that no additional 1804 Plain-4 Eagles were struck is explained by the much higher production cost due to the gold content and by the circumstance that there was a significant number of existing 1804 Crosslet-4 Eagles so the Mint did not see a reason to make more as specimens.

During the late nineteenth century, a romance developed around the 1804 silver Dollar, because collectors wondered about the whereabouts of the 19,570 coins the Mint had reportedly made. Only a few were known, and so a romantic story ensued, that most, if not all, of the 1804 silver Dollars had been shipped off to Africa to pay American soldiers and sailors engaged in the war against Tripoli. The story includes wildly quixotic references to shipwrecks, forced marches across burning deserts, and the eventual payment to seventy American seamen and a mounted force of Arabs.

Theoretically, these Dollars never returned to the United States, which explained their great rarity. The fact that no silver Dollar dated 1804 had ever been made seems not to have crossed the minds of most collectors until the twentieth century. We now know the true story, and in many ways the true tale is much more romantic than the fictional version.

Again, it needs to be mentioned that the primary emphasis over the years has been on the 1804 silver Dollars, because none were actually made in 1804, and any that turned up were true rarities. The 1804 Plain-4 Eagle, on the other hand, has been largely ignored because of all the 1804 Crosslet-4 Eagles that were in fact minted in 1804. Only in very recent times have numismatists understood the difference between the Crosslet-4 and the Plain-4 varieties of the 1804 Eagle and what an unimaginable rarity the four known specimens actually are — even in comparison to the 1804 silver Dollar.

The story of the 1804 silver Dollar has an additional twist to it that somewhat clouds the story of its origins. Collectors divide the 1804 silver Dollars into three classes. Class I consists of coins made for the diplomatic presentation sets in 1834 and 1835 (as well as additional specimens made at the same time for other purposes), but in the late

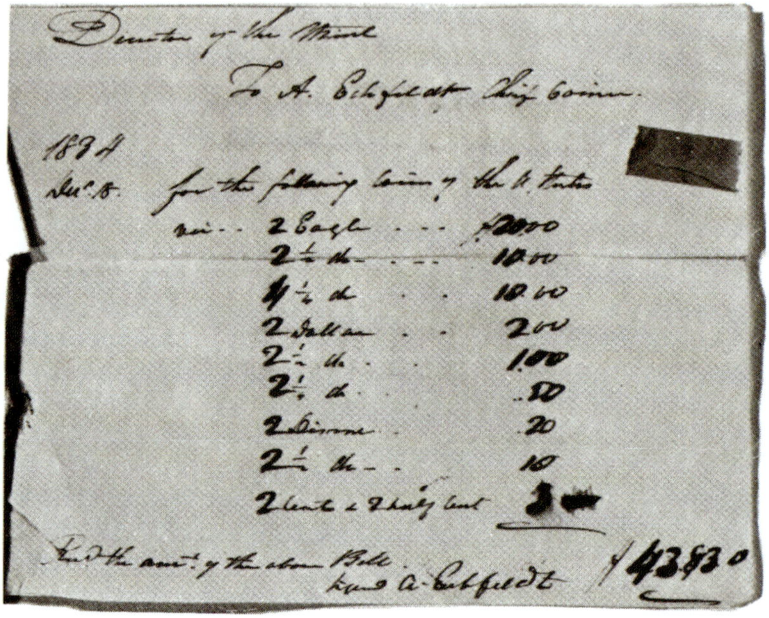
Director of the Mint
To A. Eckfeldt Chief Coiner
1834
Dec. 18 for the following coins of the U. States
viz. . 2 Eagles . . . $20.00
2 ½ do . . . 10.00
2 ¼ do . . 10.00
2 Dollars . . 2.00
2 ½ do . 1.00
2 ¼ do . .50
2 Dimes . .20
2 ½ do . . .10
2 cents & 2 half cents .03
Recd the amt. of the above Bill
A. Eckfeldt $43.83

1834 Eckfeldt Invoice for Coin Set

1850s, a small number of these 1804 silver Dollars were illegally struck at the Mint, allegedly by an employee named Theodore Eckfeldt, who was the night watchman.

Only one specimen of the Class II 1804 silver Dollar, which has no edge lettering, is known to exist. Its distinction lies in the fact that is was struck over a Swiss Shooting Thaler, dated 1857. This coin is now part of the Smithsonian Institution collection. Class III 1804 silver Dollars, which contain edge lettering, are more numerous, as there are six known examples.

All of the clandestinely struck Class II coins were sold in a Philadelphia shop owned by Dr. Montroville W. Dickeson; when Mint Director James Ross Snowden discovered their existence, every effort was made to recover them. One of the recovered pieces, the only one now known to exist, was placed in the Mint Cabinet.

Additional 1804 Dollars, this time with the properly lettered edge, were secretly struck in late 1859 or early 1860. These Class III coins, as they are now called, were laid aside to avoid detection by Director Snowden. Some years later they were quietly sold to collectors and dealers. The six Class III Dollars are probably all that were made.

FID DEF IND IMP
ONE
PENNY

CHAPTER EIGHT

DELIVERING THE COINS AND RATIFIED TREATIES

Once again, Roberts received instructions from the State Department regarding how he was to proceed in his second mission. In a letter dated March 20, 1835, Secretary of State John Forsyth wrote the following:

> You are already informed of your appointment as Agent on the part of the government to exchange the ratification of treaties recently concluded with the King of Siam and the Sultan of Muscat, and to make such commercial arrangement with other powers whose dominions border upon the Indian Ocean, as may lead to the advancement or security of the commerce of the United States in that quarter. You are also apprised that the Sloop of War *Peacock* will be at New York, in readiness to receive you, on the 25th of the present month.
>
> I now proceed to state to you more distinctly the objects of your mission, and the means of effecting them which will be placed at your disposal, together with such instructions as are thought proper in respect to the mode of proceeding. The articles intended as presents to be distributed upon the exchange of ratifications with the governments of Siam and Muscat are stored in the city of New York, [everything] in complete order for shipping; and the necessary directions are herewith sent, addressed to William M. Price Esq., the agent by whom they were purchased, for the delivery of them into your possession.

The ratified treaties are transmitted to you by the bearer of this dispatch.

Immediately upon receiving them you will embark on the *Peacock*, which will convey you by way of the Cape of Good Hope, to Muscat and thence to Siam. At these places you will effect the exchange of ratifications, with as much expedition as may be expected on the occasion, in the manner denoted in this list which accompanies these instructions, and apprising the respective sovereigns of the friendly feelings entertained toward them by the people of the United States, and of the satisfaction with which the conclusion of the recent treaties regarded by the President as tending to cherish the amicable relations between the parties and to promote their mutual prosperities.

From Siam you will proceed to Cochin China and use every endeavor, consistent with the dignity of the government and with the means afforded you, to form a commercial treaty with that country. In the efforts you are expected to make for the accomplishments of the object, much must necessarily be left to your own discretion. Everything has been done by the government that suggests itself as likely to facilitate your negotiations, with a people possessing habits and feelings peculiar to the East and far different from our own. You will have at your disposal such an amount of presents as has been thought necessary to proceed with negotiations, which you will distribute in such way as you may think most conducive to your success: and you are also furnished with a power to treat, and with a letter from the President to the Emperor, in preparation of which regard has been had to the ideas of the nation for which it is intended, in respect to the ceremony which should characterize all intercourse with the sovereign. Observing the same policy, you will of course accommodate yourself to the peculiar notions and customs of the country, however absurd they may be, wherever you can do so without such an acknowledgment of inferiority as would be incompatible with the dignity of your own government, of which you will on all occasions assert the equality with the most powerful nations of the world.

You will studiously inculcate upon all those with whom you have intercourse the particular situation, character, and views of this country: that it is an essential part of our policy to avoid political connections with any other government; that although we are a powerful nation, possessing great resources, an extensive trade, and a large fleet, all our past history shows that we are not ambitious of conquest: that we desire no colonial possessions: that we seek a free and friendly intercourse with all the world: and that our interests and inclinations alike lead us to deprecate a state of war with any nation, except in self-defense or as a vindication of our own violated rights or honor. You will point out, where it may be necessary, the difference which exists between ourselves and other nations in these respects; and endeavor to remove the fears and prejudices which may have been generated by the encroachments or aggressions of European powers.

From Cochin China you will pass on to Japan in relation to which you will conform to the instructions that have now been given you in respect to the former. As the Dutch have their factory at Nagasaki, and might feel themselves interested in thwarting your mission, it is recommended that, if permitted, you should enter some other port nearer to the seat of government — that of Omari will hereby be found the most eligible — in order to facilitate your negotiations with this government, the same documents are furnished you as in the case of Cochin China, together with suitable presents for the Emperor and inferior officers.

If you should deem it essential toward concluding a treaty with either or both of the countries in question, you are authorized to promise additional presents when the exchange of ratifications, not to exceed in either case the value of ten thousand dollars, but to be proportioned in some measure according to the liberality of the provisions in favor of the United States which may be combined in restrictive treaties. Through the whole process of this business you will use all the dispersed which may be consistent with its faithful and prudent execution, and as soon as it is terminated, whether personally or otherwise, you will return to the United States in the same vessel which takes you out and will proceed to this city without delay.

You will keep the Department constantly acquainted with your proceedings as far as your opportunities may enable you to do it; and communicate information from time to time to what points dispatches, addressed to you should be directed, in case there should be instructions to forward. You will keep a minute and accurate journal of the events of your mission, including a register of your own observations of such important information as you may collect respecting the population, introductions, trade, customs, and character of the countries you may visit, which you will deposit in the Department for the use of the government when you return. (Bowers, pp. 196–97)

The last paragraph dealt with Roberts's compensation — $4,400 a year — and a postscript telling him that he was at liberty to change his routes if the necessity arose. One interesting side note is that the Japanese wanted to acquire some sheep from which woolen cloth could be made, but their principal trading partner, the Dutch, would not comply with this request, and thus it was decided to send some sheep with Roberts for the Japanese emperor as a way to get the United States' proverbial foot in the door.

GIFTS GALORE

The official list of gifts that Roberts was to distribute to the various Eastern rulers was extensive. For Siam, there were six crates of lamps valued at $2,750 (presumably the cut-glass lamps on the king's wish list), five crates of Nankeen cotton cloth, $400 worth of carpeting purchased at the Looking Glass and Carpet Warehouse in Boston, a crate of men's clothing destined for both Muscat and Siam, and a crate of women's clothing from Miss Ann Maria Wittingham. Wittingham did business on Broadway in New York City, and later her establishment became known as "Wittingham's Fancy Store" and was operated by William Wittingham.

In addition, the king of Siam was to receive two crates of mirrors valued at $600, two flags, two boxes of shawls, two maps, a number of swords, carbines, and rifles, a package of pictures, and, of course, the package of coins. The sultan of Muscat, on the other hand, was not so lavishly gifted. He was to receive three crates of lamps valued at $550, three boxes of Nankeen cloth, one flag, one map, two swords, and one package of all-important coins.

For Cochin China, Roberts was given a gold watch with a heavy chain that was eight feet long, a music box, four pieces of superior-quality broadcloth (each twenty yards long in scarlet, blue, brown, and light green), fifty yards of orange or yellow silk velvet, a set of cut glass, including six decanters and four dozen tumblers, goblets, and wine glasses, a set of prints featuring American naval victories, a map of the United States, a trunk containing specimens of American cotton merchandise, a crescent-form saber, a rifle, a shotgun, a supply of percussion caps, a pair of pistols, and a case of U.S. coins like the ones taken to Siam and Muscat.

Japan was to receive the aforementioned ten Merino sheep (two rams and eight ewes), four canisters of saffron (about thirty pounds), a repeating gold watch with an eight-foot-long chain, a music box, five pieces of superior-quality broadcloth (each twenty yards long in red, yellow, green, dark blue, and light blue), a cut-glass dessert set, a map of the United States, a set of American naval victory prints, a trunk containing specimens of American cotton merchandise, a crescent-form saber, a rifle, a shotgun, a supply of percussion caps, a pair of pistols in a case — and, again, a set of American coins.

ROBERTS'S SECOND VOYAGE BEGINS

In order to take Roberts and all of the diplomatic gifts back to the Near and Far East, the sloop of war *U.S.S. Peacock* was chosen once again and relieved of its others duties, which mainly consisted of transporting free American Negroes to Liberia on the coast of West Africa. This time, however, the *Boxer* was not the escort vessel — that role was taken by the *U.S.S. Enterprise*. Together the two ships were referred to rather grandiosely as the "East India and Asiatic Squadron."

It was anticipated that the voyage would take more than two years to complete and would circumnavigate the globe. The *Peacock* left New York harbor on April 23, 1835, a Friday, on its way to Rio de Janeiro to join with the *Enterprise*. The *Peacock* was well armed, with twenty thirty-two-pound cannons and two long-range twelve-pounders. It was considered a "wet ship," meaning that in heavy seas when the ship was laboring the seams tended to open up and let in water.

On May 28, the ship crossed the equator — an event generally called "crossing the line." Although not noted in the ship's log, this was probably a time of frivolity, during which those on board who had never "crossed the line" (called "pollywogs") were initiated by those who had (called "shellbacks"). This probably began as a semirough time for the pollywogs, who had to run the gauntlet, but it ended with celebration, hilarity, and hijinks.

Land was sighted on June 10, 1835, and on June 11, the *Peacock* sailed into Rio de Janeiro harbor. This turned into something of a cannonade when the *Peacock* saluted the town with seventeen guns, and the town returned the honor with a nineteen-gun salute. This was followed by a fifteen-gun salute to the French and British admirals who were also in port, and they returned with the same number of guns. This must have sounded like a small naval battle in progress.

These salutes continued for days while the *Peacock* was in port, because the ship was regularly visited by various admirals and diplomatic personnel. While in port, the ship had twenty-one caulkers come on board to help with the "wetness problem," and they worked from June 22 to July 5 to try to alleviate the situation. At the same time, painters were hard at work, and the ship was being refitted and resupplied. The ship was also rewatered, which means that a $24 fee was paid for a large tank containing 12,000 to 14,000 gallons of water to be floated out to the ship and off-loaded.

The *Peacock* and the *Enterprise* sailed on July 12, but it was soon decided that the schooner *Enterprise* was "an indifferent sailer," and it was decided that the two ships would not keep close company. That night, the two vessels separated, with the *Peacock* sailing ahead of the *Enterprise* toward its next port of call — Zanzibar.

After some difficulty (such as brushing against shoals and scraping the bottom of the ship over uncharted reefs) reaching the Zanzibar coast, the *Peacock* saw a strange-looking "canoe" (probably a dhow) approach the ship, which was paddled by a Negro who just happened to be completely naked. His passenger in the odd vessel was an Arab wearing nothing more than a large turban and a waist band (a loin cloth?). The Arab climbed up the side of the *Peacock* and announced that he was the Zanzibar harbor pilot. As for his credentials, he took a pasteboard box (labeled "Lucifer matches") out from under his turban, but inside were written testimonials from various American and European ships' captains about what an experienced, safe pilot he was.

Once aboard the *Peacock*, the pilot, whose name was Hassan ben Seid, squatted on the taffrail (the rail around the stern of a wooden ship). To the ship's surgeon, he looked like a frog, but he (the pilot) began chewing tobacco and giving hand signals for directions through the dangerous waters. The ship anchored around sunset off the sultan's palace at Metony (or Mtony), which was about three miles north of the town of Zanzibar.

The governor of Zanzibar (the approximately sixteen-year-old son of the sultan of Muscat) sent the *Peacock* a lavish gift of food, including fruit, poultry, and goats. In his journal of the voyage, the ship's surgeon notes the range of the sultan of Muscat's dominion and gives a glimpse of why he was thought to be so important to the American commerce of the day:

> The dominions of the Sultan of Muscat are not very clearly defined though they are of very considerable extent. On the coast of Africa, he claims all the coast and circumjacent islands from Cape Delgado [modern-day northeast Mozambique], situated in 10 degrees south latitude, to Cape Guardafui [modern-day Somalia — the cape is the apex of the so-called Horn of Africa], in eleven degrees and fifty minutes north. In this range, we find the ports of Monghow, or Mongalow, Lyndy, Mombassa, Quiloa, Melinda, Lamo, Patta, Brava, Modkesha, or Magodosh [the Magadoxa of the Portuguese], and the islands of Mafeea, Mowfea, Zanzibar, Pemba, Socotra, etc.
>
> In southern and eastern Arabia, the Sultan claims the coast, from Cape Aden to Cape Ras el Had; thence northward as far as Bassorah, in latitude 29 [degrees and] 30 [minutes] north, all the coast and islands of

> the Persian Gulf, including the pearl fishery and islands of Barhein [Bahrain], as far as Sinde, on the eastern side. All this extent of territory is not garrisoned by his troops, but is considered to be tributary to him. He rents besides, sulfur mines in Persia, and several estates in Gambroon.
>
> The commercial value of these possessions, and the revenue derived from them, we have no means of ascertaining. The pearl fisheries of Barhein we once estimated to be worth annually more than three millions of pounds sterling; but at present it does not probably yield one-tenth of that sum. The fishing season lasts from April until October, and extends over a space of 12 to 15 miles. Arabs are the only people engaged in it. (Bowers 1999, 224)

After taking on fresh provisions that were provided at no expense by the sultan, the *Peacock* left Zanzibar on September 8, 1835. The *Enterprise*, which had been trailing far behind the *Peacock*, did not arrive in Zanzibar until September 14 and sailed once again on September 20 with the idea that both ships would rendezvous in Muscat before they sailed into the much more dangerous waters around Siam and Cochin-China.

IN SHALLOW WATER BUT DEEP TROUBLE

Then, disaster struck — or near disaster. On Tuesday morning, September 22, the *Peacock* ran aground a coral reef. Roberts recorded a dramatic account of this calamity in a letter to his children, dated October 22, 1835:

> An almost fatal disaster befell us between 2 and 3 o'clock in the morning when we were reposing as we supposed in perfect security in our cots, in fine weather, every sail being set on the ship that would draw, and going at the rate of nine miles per hour.
>
> Suddenly, the most appalling sounds saluted our ears, resembling tremendous and continued shocks of an earthquake, making the ship tremble like the disjointed or tearing asunder of a mighty fabric, for the ship was stranded in an extensive coral reef near to the island of Mazeira

> on the desolate coast of Arabia, to the northward of what is called Arabia Felix on the coast of Hadzamant. (Bowers 1999, 225)

The island about which Roberts was writing is now most commonly called "Masirah," but over the years the spelling of its name has changed many times. Roberts spelled it "Mazeira," but nineteenth-century maps used "Moseirah" or "Massera." Regardless of how it is spelled, it is a rather desolate desert island that today has a population of less than 10,000 and is hard to reach except by Omani military aircraft or a ferry. It is known for its fisheries and its world-class surfing.

Masirah Island is located in the Indian Ocean off the coast of southern Oman, and it is south of the "Horn of Africa." It is approximately 65 kilometers long and varies between 6 and 18 kilometers wide. Unfortunately, it is unclear how to translate Roberts's reference to the "coast of Hadzamant" into modern terms.

Roberts continues the letter to his children by discussing how this might have happened:

> The day previous our three chronometers placed us 72 miles to the eastward of M. [Mazeira], and it was intended to preserve this distance by keeping on a north course. We cannot even now account for this disaster unless an error occurred in the observations for the correction of the chronometers as the atmosphere at the time was very hazy, the longitude of the island was placed too far to the westward, and we were also powerfully affected by the current settling into the Gulf of Mazeira. (Bowers 1999, 227)

The question was, were they shipwrecked, or could the ship be saved? The crew worked frantically, and they lightened the ship by discarding all but 2,500 gallons of water and 250 gallons of whiskey. They threw overboard all of the spare jars, spare chains, and sheet cable. They jettisoned much of their heavy projectiles, such as grape shot, canisters, and round shot. They then constructed a raft and put on it much of their foodstuffs and essential materials such as resin and tar.

When this did not lighten the ship enough, the sailors began pushing the cannons overboard, but then a fleet of pirates showed up hoping to destroy the surviving crew and to begin a salvage operation. Roberts continues with his narrative, which begins to read something like an adventure novel:

> The instant the ship struck, the helm was put hard to port, so as to throw her head to the eastward, but it was ineffectual for she was immovable excepting occasionally when she struck either forward or abaft when she descended into the hollow of the sea. The sea at that time was fortunately not violent, and we ascertained shortly by the stillness of the ship that the tide was ebbing. When daylight appeared, we found ourselves within a mile and a half of a low sandy island having on it a few bushes. After two ineffectual attempts to heave the ship off into deep water, and expecting that she would go to pieces [in] the first gale on a coast where no succor could be had short of Muscat, a distance of 400 miles — being beset by a great number of piratical dows [dhows] who plundered our raft made of the ship's spare parts and on which were placed barrels of provisions, naval stores, etc., etc., and they made also a very bold attempt to cut off the launch and first cutter in which, had they succeeded, the ship would have been lost, and we should have been deprived of the means of carrying our anchors to heave off the ship.
>
> The pirates were accumulating a large force for the purpose of destroying us and making a prize of the vessel. The ship's boats were insufficient to save one-third of the crew and conduct them either to Bombay or Muscat. Matters being placed in this critical and painful situation, I volunteered my services to proceed to Muscat in a small open boat (being the 2nd cutter of 20 feet in length) to procure aid and assistance from the Sultan.
>
> At daylight on the 22nd I left the ship, accompanied by Midshipman W. R. Taylor and six men, on this perilous enterprise, against numerous pirates, and the dangers of the ocean. We were chased upwards of five hours that day by a pirate dow [dhow], to the distance of 25 miles, but darkness coming on favored our escape. The same night the boat was all but lost in a heavy sea by being nearly filled with water.

> I had intended to mention previously that if the piratical vessel had come up with us, we should have given him a warm reception with our musketry, and then pulled the boat immediately to windward. Finally, if we could not have succeeded in beating her off, then to have given them another volley of musketry and boarded her with our cutlasses and pistols, and made a prize of her if possible. I am satisfied that not a man in the boat would have submitted so long as he could have wielded an arm in his defense, for death awaited us if taken, and it was much better to have died with arms in our hands, fighting for self-preservation, than basely to have submitted to ignominious death. (Bowers 1999, 227)

While Roberts was concerned about imminent death, the crew seemed to be more worried about being taken prisoners and then put into slavery to bedouin Arabs. Luckily, the exertions of the crew finally paid off, and the ship made it back into deep water. The pirates did, however, manage to steal part of the contents of the raft, but they were then dissuaded by musket and cannon fire.

When Roberts left the besieged vessel, it is reported that he took the ratified treaty with him — but he surely left behind the precious gifts for the sultan. It can only be imagined what might have happened to this precious cargo — and the four 1804 Plain-4 Eagles — if the pirates had succeeded and captured the *Peacock*.

Meanwhile, the small boat carrying Roberts and the accompanying sailors from the *Peacock* arrived in Muscat after a little more than four days at sea. They stopped short of the city in a small bay to wait for daylight so that they would not run past the city in the darkness. They had a dwindling water supply, and their food consisted of only a little "damaged bread." Roberts arrived exhausted, sunburned, and blistered — but alive.

The *Peacock* was sailing behind them, but the vessel was taking on a reported twelve to fourteen inches of water each hour in the hold. The sailors were manning the pumps with gusto, but they were exhausted from their ordeal and lack of sleep.

In Muscat, Roberts wasted no time finding an interpreter and going to see the sultan, who was very sympathetic and accommodating. Should the *Peacock* prove to be ultimately lost, the sultan promised to provide two ships — one to repatriate the crew to the United States and the other to take Roberts on the rest of his mission and then deliver him back to the United States.

While the fate of the *Peacock* was being determined, the sultan offered to provide Roberts with a house in the city for his comfort or a cabin on one of the sultan's larger ships. The latter location was offered because the city was stiflingly hot, and it was cooler on the water onboard the ship. Roberts refused both offers of accommodations and stayed with Captain Sayed bin Caffaun, the sultan's interpreter.

The sultan mounted a full-fledged rescue effort by dispatching his flagship, the *Sultane*, with water and food to Mazeira Island to assist the *Peacock*. He also sent to Zoar, a large town near Ras al Had (a cape on the Horn of Africa), orders to send four dhows and 300 men to protect the crew and property onboard the *Peacock* until the *Sultane* could arrive. He supplied the governor of Zoar (about 100 mile southwest of Muscat) with an American flag that the dhows could fly and a letter from Roberts so there would be no confusing them with the pirates.

Then the sultan sent messengers to the governor of Mazeira and the principal bedouin chiefs of the area to relate that if any crew members were harmed or any property was lost, they would be held responsible — and it would mean their heads. It must be assumed that the sultan was completely serious, and that any disobedience would be met with a visit from his executioner.

The *Sultane* intercepted the *Peacock* the day before the American ship reached the safe harbor at Muscat. The Omanis sent over gifts of food — fruit, dates, goats, and cebu (also spelled zebu, Asian/Africa humped bovines) — and then escorted the badly leaking *Peacock* into Muscat harbor.

SUCCESS IN MUSCAT

What did Americans hope to sell in the Middle East with the trade treaty? Well, Oman and Muscat were the gateway to the Persian Gulf, the Red Sea, and the East Coast of Africa, and American interests wanted primarily to sell cotton, which was preferred in that part of the world (particularly in Persia) to English cloth. Part of the plan was to store items made in America in Muscat to be transshipped to other parts of the Arab and Persian world under the sultan's control.

Other than cotton, the Omani were interested in importing woolen goods, rice, iron, lead, and sugar. For export from the various regions under the sultan's control there were such exotic goods as ivory, tortoise shell, rhinoceros hides and horns, and various substances used for medicinal purposes, along with more mundane things such as dates, wheat, raisins, salted and dried fish, coffee, beeswax, coconut oil, aloe, and the famous Arabian horses.

In a letter to Secretary of State Forsyth, Roberts reports that during the period September 16, 1832–May 26, 1835, forty-one foreign ships visited the harbor at Zanzibar, of which the vast majority, thirty-two, were American vessels. Seven were British, one was French, and the last one was Spanish.

Roberts continues by reporting that with the new treaty the American ships will have a great advantage if they intend to pay for the goods they purchase with either gold or silver. He goes on to say that there are no anchorage fees for such transactions and that the ship pays no other duties or charges except 5 percent on merchandise. Foreign ships, however, have to pay 5 percent going into the harbor and 5 percent leaving the harbor, plus an anchorage fee. This was quite a good deal for the Americans.

Fortunately, all of the diplomatic goods had survived the *Peacock*'s troubles, and, of course, as previously stated, Roberts carried the all-important ratified treaty with him during his emergency trip in the open boat. The treaties were exchanged with the sultan on September 30, 1835, with one small snafu — the sultan had left his official copy in Zanzibar, and instead of having to take the long trip to fetch it, Roberts made another copy.

On October 1, the diplomatic presents came ashore to be presented to the sultan. The ship's surgeon, W. S. W. Ruschenberger, was a little dismissive of the gifts and listed them rather perfunctorily as if they were of little importance. He related that the gold sword, previously mentioned, was made in New York City, along with "Tanner's map of the United States" — presumably Henry Schenck Tanner's United States of America, which was first printed as a wall map in 1829.

Ruschenberger went on to list an American flag (we know the sultan already had one of these), "several rifles, a number of cut-glass lamps, a quantity of American nankin, known as Forsyth's nankin." It can only be assumed that the good doctor was referring to the firm of William Forsyth and Company, which was an importer of nankeen fabric into North America. Although the sources are vague on this point, this company appears to have been Canadian (references are to business being conducted in Nova Scotia), and the origin of the fabric itself was China or East India.

In the middle of this list is the notation "a set of American coins." There is no mention whatsoever how special this set was, and how important it would be in later years, and no mention of any presents the sultan might have sent to President Jackson, except that it is repeatedly noted that taking presents from a foreign power or sovereign was expressly forbidden by American constitutional law. In any event, the sultan did send large quantities of food and supplies to the *Peacock*.

The only remaining question was, when would the treaty with Muscat go into effect? The sultan did not seem to care, but Roberts wanted it to be retroactive and to be placed in force as of June 30, 1834, the day the U.S. Senate ratified the treaty. The only problem the sultan had with that date was that it meant certain fees and duties paid at Zanzibar between June 30, 1834, and October 1835 would have to be refunded to American ships, because the new treaty had a fee structure lower than was in effect at the earlier time.

The sultan really did not care all that much, because the collections of fees and duties in Zanzibar were farmed out to a private company, and they would have to make the refund and suffer the loss — not the government of Muscat. This prompted him to accept the date Roberts favored, and the American diplomat saw that as something of a victory for American commercial interests. Having completed its business, the *Peacock* — somewhat the worse for wear — sailed for Siam late Saturday, October 10, 1835.

CHAPTER NINE

Siam and Tragedy

On their voyage toward Siam, the presence of Halley's comet in the sky is noted in the ship's log without much fanfare. In past centuries, this apparition in the sky has been associated with dire happenings, and for Edmund Roberts, this tragic tradition sadly came to fruition.

SOJOURN IN BOMBAY

As the ship was off Mumbai (or Bombay), India, Roberts wrote his future plans to Secretary of State Forsyth, saying that he planned to finish up in Siam, push on to Cochin China, and arrive in Canton by June 1836. He planned to go from there to Japan, but the old proverb, about man proposing and God disposing, came into play.

Once in Bombay, the *Peacock* found that its erstwhile escort ship, the *Enterprise*, had finally caught up with it. This was a good opportunity for repairs, and the *Peacock* was put into the East India Company's drydock for a much-needed going over. While the ship was out of the water, Roberts and some of the ship's officers rented a house in town while Commodore Kennedy, the overall commander of the expedition, moved his "flag" (a pennant signifying the presence of the overall fleet leader) and his command from the *U.S.S. Peacock* to the *U.S.S. Enterprise*. The *Peacock*'s crew was reportedly housed on the *U.S.S. Hastings*.

The *Peacock* was found to be in rather poor condition — it needed to be recaulked, to have its bottom recoppered, and to have a new false keel added. (A keel, incidentally, is the large beam around which a ship is built, and a "false keel" on wooden ships was a timber attached to the underside of the main keel by iron staples. The false keel was meant to protect the heads of bolts holding the main keel together and also to protect this vital structure from damage. The false keel also increased a ship's stability.)

In early November, the sultan of Muscat once again proved that he was a very good friend to the Americans. At that time, a ship from Muscat arrived in Bombay carrying the eleven cannons that the *Peacock* had jettisoned during its troubles off of Mazeira Island. The Americans had left marker buoys where the cannons had been thrown overboard, and the sultan had had them raised from the bottom of the Indian Ocean. He then had the weapons transported to Bombay — all at his own expense.

Reprovisioned, repaired, and refitted, the *Peacock* and the *Enterprise* left Bombay on December 4, 1835, on their way to Colombo, Ceylon (modern Sri Lanka) to refill their water supply, since the water in Bombay was thought not to be healthy. Ominously, the ship's surgeon notes that the crew got sick from drinking the Bombay water and from the unhealthy (marshy) atmosphere, and he states that at any given time, as many as one quarter of the crew was on the sick list.

The *Peacock* arrived in Ceylon on December 16 and took on fresh drinking water. Roberts and the officers engaged in a great deal of sightseeing, such as watching a mongoose (about the size of a kitten) kill a cobra, and then the ship sailed on Christmas Eve. Christmas was not a widely celebrated holiday in 1835 America.

Christmas was thought by many to be a Catholic celebration, and Protestant Americans tended to ignore it. In fact, New England's Puritans had outlawed Christmas in Boston during part of the seventeenth century, and Congress was actually in session on December 25, 1789 —

the first Christmas the U.S. Constitution was in force. Christmas did not become a federally recognized holiday until 1870, but the captain of the *Peacock* did give the crew a holiday for the occasion. (New Year's Day, however, was not celebrated.)

THAT TERRIBLE SCOURGE OF ARMIES AND SAILORS

The *Peacock* sailed on toward Siam through January, February, and March, but in February death became a passenger. The first to die was a wardroom cook, William Lewis, and the second was Charles Fisher, a seaman and wardroom cook. These were the first deaths aboard the *Peacock*, and the ship's surgeon Ruschenberger notes that "that terrible scourge of armies, and sailors, dysentery, made its appearance on board."

The Gulf of Siam was entered on March 20, and on the 24th, Special Envoy Roberts sent a letter announcing his arrival to the king of Siam. He told the king that he had the ratified treaty and wanted to exchange it for the Siamese version that carried the royal seal and the necessary certificate of ratification.

Roberts went on to say that he had the gifts requested by his majesty, except for the stone statues that could not be obtained, and the various trees, seeds, and plants, because these had perished during the journey as they were thrown overboard during the difficulty off of Mazeira Island. Roberts said he hoped this shortcoming would be made up for by extra "elegant and expensive lamps" and other unmentioned items.

The king was asked to send a boat to receive the diplomatic gifts plus other boats to bring to him Roberts and his party (about twenty-five people) with the treaty. Roberts failed to mention that the treaty he was delivering was in a mutilated condition and was in need of repair due to the problems off of Mazeira Island.

The *Peacock* found itself on March 28 off Meinam River, where it was visited by the heir apparent, who was the king's half brother. Ruschenberger refers to him as "Prince Momfanoi," which he translates as "Prince of Heaven, Junior" — actually "the younger" would have been more accurate.

The "Meinam" River, or "Mae Nam" River, means "Mother of Waters," and it is now better known as the Chao Phranya, or River of Kings. It empties into the Gulf of Siam (Thailand), about twenty miles west of Bangkok, and is a very important waterway in Siam.

Before visiting the king, Roberts thought it polite to make as many visits as possible to local officials. To do so, he and his party dressed in their best uniforms and clothes and had the ship's band precede them wherever they were going. The idea behind this procession was that, while in the East, they should exercise all of the pomp and circumstance that could possibly be mustered to impress perceived Asian sensibilities.

In his commentary on the voyage, Ruschenberger noted, "The chief merchants in Siam are the King, his ministers, the Chinese, and old women" (Bowers 1999, 264). What did the Americans hope to sell in Siam? Various cotton goods were at the top of the list, and it was mentioned that American cottons demanded a good price because they were found to be very durable. In addition, the list included military arms and some equipment and glassware — which seems rather odd, because the American glass industry was really in its infancy at the time. In exchange, the Americans hoped to buy from Siam primarily sugar, tin, various kinds of wood, drugs, and rattan.

Unfortunately, the Americans did not get everything they wanted in this treaty. One of the main things desired by Washington was the right to a consul in Siam, which was not agreed to by the Siamese. The United States also wanted to trade in rice, but that too was rejected. (See the Appendix, which is the text of the treaty between Siam and the United States.) The diplomatic party was delayed in traveling to Bangkok, and the ship was in need of water and new provisions. As time stretched on, the ship's surgeon Ruschenberger and a companion tried to slip into Bangkok to secure water and food. Before arriving, they visited the governor of Paknam, who explained to them that if they did indeed proceed to Bangkok that he would have his head cut off as punishment, and the good feeling toward the Americans would come to an abrupt end.

Ruschenberger described Paknam as being the "vilest, dirtiest, the most inhospitable and detestable spot I have ever set foot in." The good doctor was particularly disturbed at finding the governor lounging around four-fifths naked and smoking opium, surrounded by slaves and low-ranking attendants. He was sixty-four years old, and while the Americans were there his granddaughters came in the room clad only in golden filigree "fig leaves," attached around their waist with gold chains. The little girls entered the room and began smoking cigars, and the comment was made that even infants were given tobacco before they were weaned.

The party was asked to spend the night and was provided with mattresses patched with velvet, but the lights in the room were never extinguished, and all of the attendants stayed and talked. Ruschenberger speaks of the barking dogs, the yowling cats, and the lizards scurrying across the floor — and, finally, he and his party fled (literally) back to the *Peacock* at 4 a.m., mission *not* accomplished.

It was not until April 5 that the boats arrived to take the diplomatic mission into Bangkok to meet with the king. The ship was seriously short of water and provisions, and rationing was being considered. The Americans were more than a little put out with the Siamese, because they felt the long delay in being received was an insult, especially in light of another American ship that arrived in harbor, well after the *Peacock* had been given permission to proceed almost immediately.

The diplomatic mission on the *Peacock* had been made to wait from March 28 to April 5, but the interpreter explained that this should be considered a great honor being paid to the dignity of the Americans.

He went on to explain that the longer the Americans were made to wait, the longer the Siamese would have to prepare to welcome them with pomp and circumstance, and the greater the compliment.

When the Siamese boat arrived to transport the Americans to the capital, it also brought a gift of fruit and water to help with the supply problems. Twenty officers, plus servants, and the ship's band departed the *Peacock* on the Siamese ship, and along with them went the cargo of presents. Roberts listed the six cut-glass lamps, the nankeens, the carpeting, male and female American-style clothing, two large mirrors, an American flag, a map, and shawls. Two other gifts — the two swords with the gold scabbards and the set of Proof coins containing the precious 1804 Plain-4 Proof Eagle — were transported by Roberts himself, and he kept these close to his person.

Roberts, on April 12, had his first interview with the king or "rajah" of Lagor, who had been appointed by the king of Siam to settle the issue of how the regal seal of Siam was to be affixed to the treaty itself or to the certificate of ratification. Lagor is often associated with the city of Nakhon Si Thammarat, on the east coast of the Malay Peninsula and 610 miles south of Bangkok.

It is one of the most ancient cities in Siam and was capital of Tambralinga, or the kingdom of Lagor (Ligor). It served as the southern administrative capital of Siam and was considered a tributary state. Besides being called a "rajah" the king of Lagor was also called a "viceroy," meaning that he was the governor of the province. He was certainly subservient to his "Magnificent Majesty," the king of Siam.

The king of Lagor wanted to affix the seals to the certificate of ratification only, but Roberts objected to this, saying that the king (of Siam) had originally agreed to affix the seal to the articles of the treaty itself as well as the certificate of ratification, and without this formality, the terms of the treaty would be invalid. The king of Lagor resisted, but Roberts eventually got his way.

POMP AND CEREMONY

When the day came to transfer the American-ratified treaty to the Siamese, the king sent a large boat (which the Americans insisted on calling a "canoe"). It was eighty feet long and was propelled by thirty-four oars, and over its center was a gold-embroidered scarlet silk canopy. The oars were manned by thirty-four men, impressively adorned in the red uniform of the king of Siam, a very striking sight. The ceremony began with Roberts marching approximately 100 yards toward the river with the treaty and accompanied by the band from the *Peacock*:

King Rama III of Siam

> On reaching the margin of the river Mr. Roberts took the Treaty in his hand, and, after holding it up above his head in token of respect, delivered it to a Siamese officer, the secretary of the P'hra Klang [diplomatic minister]. He also held it above his head, and then, shaded by a royal chat, a large white silk umbrella, borne by a slave, passed it into the boat, where it was received upon an ornamental stand, and after covering it with a cone of gilt paper, it was placed beneath the canopy. At this moment our band ceased, and that of the Siamese began to play. The canoe shoved off, and we turned our steps homeward to the merry tune of Yankee Doodle." (Bowers 1999, 264)

Finally, on April 16, the Americans were brought into the presence of King Rama III (aka Ph'ra Nang Klao). His Magnificent Majesty was described as an obese man weighing an estimated minimum of 300 pounds and a maximum of 420. He was found sitting cross-legged on his diamond-studded golden throne (how a man that large managed to sit cross-legged in a chair is open to some conjecture).

When the party approached, the king was chewing on areca (sometimes called "betel" nut) and spitting the juice into a golden urn, which means that the king, like many of his less-lordly subjects, must have had very dark teeth because of the staining caused by the red juice of the areca. In Thai, areca is called "mahk," and it was widely used as a stimulant, although it is said to be about as strong as caffeine or nicotine.

The king is said to have been wearing a mantle of "gold tissue," and somewhere on his person (it is not explained where), he was wearing diamonds that twinkled in the subdued lighting. The Americans bowed three times, as they had done before when coming into the presence of the king, and then they sat on the floor, careful to place their feet underneath them, pointed away from the king, who would have been greatly offended by the soles of their shoes. Everyone else was barefoot in the king's presence, except the Americans.

Once seated, the Americans gave the king three Thai salaams, while the rest of the large crowd in the room knocked their head against the floor three times. Little of substance was accomplished at this meeting except small talk and the presentation of the American diplomatic gifts.

On April 18 the Siamese copy, with the attached royal seals and certificate of ratification, was delivered to the Americans with much pomp and ceremony.

> About one p.m., Mr. Roberts was informed that the golden barges of the King were in sight. Accompanied by the officers in full dress and the band, he repaired to the vessel of ceremony where he found the Phya-pi-pat-kosa had already arrived. There were three long barges, richly gilded, decorated with pennants, and each rowed by one hundred oars. The cur-

> tains were of cloth of gold with a scarlet background. That which bore the Treaty led the van. The Treaty was in a box, covered with coarse yellow silk interwoven with gold. This was placed on a silver dish, which rested on a salver with a high foot of the same metal. Over it hung a scarlet canopy, itself shaded by a royal chat [umbrella]. The scarlet uniforms of the men, and the measured stroke of the hundred oars; the flaunting banners, the music of their pipes and drums, and the glitter of gold and silver in the sun, formed a pretty pageant, and indicated with what scrupulous ceremony everything is conducted at the Magnificent Court of Siam.
>
> As the casket was raised, the Siamese band played plaintively and soft. The Phya-pi-pat-kosa conveyed it to Mr. Roberts, at the same time making a salaam, to the royal seal, attached to the Treaty. Mr. Roberts received it, and, in respect to the King, raised it as high as his head, at the same time our band struck up "Hail Columbia!" He [Roberts] then placed it upon a stand which had been provided, and deposited it in the cabin of the junk of ceremony. (Bowers 1999, 267)

With this ceremony complete, the junk of ceremony weighed anchor at midnight and started making its way down river toward the *Peacock*. By noon the next day (April 19), the crew had made it as far as Paknam.

CENT
1896
1923
TRVST

CHAPTER TEN

THE UNTIMELY END OF THE MISSION

While the American diplomatic mission was completing its tasks in Bangkok, things were not well aboard the *Peacock*. Asiatic cholera had come to the ship, and two crew members had died. It was also reported that Commodore Kennedy, the overall commander of the small fleet, was sick, but the exact nature of his illness was not made clear.

Cholera — sometimes called "Asiatic cholera" or "epidemic cholera" — is caused by the gram-negative bacterium *Vibrio cholerae*, and when this organism enters the human body (usually water- or food-borne), death can ensue within one hour of the onset of symptoms. People die from dehydration caused by a massive episode of diarrhea. According to novelist Susan Sontag, cholera can cause diarrhea and dehydration so severe that the victim of this horrific disease could literally become a wizened caricature of his or her former self before death.

When the diplomatic mission reached the *Peacock* on April 20, 1836, it was reported that all crew members were sick — and some very seriously. At sunset, the Americans sailed, and the ship was described as being "almost a hospital." Indicated on the ship's log for April 26 was that the food was going bad, with 920 pounds of bread and 30 gallons of beans having to be thrown overboard. The number of sick onboard continued to increase.

On May 2, a seaman died from dysentery and diarrhea and was buried at sea. Dysentery is also called the "flux," or the "bloody flux," and like cholera, severe diarrhea is one of its major symptoms. On May 7, all of the bread was found to be inedible and was thrown overboard, leaving the crew only salted meat and rice to eat.

It was reported by the ship's surgeon, Ruschenberger, that one fourth of the crew was confined to its hammocks, and the rest of the crew was not strong enough to truly handle the ship in any kind of emergency such as rough weather or bad seas. Still, the *Peacock* did manage to keep sailing, and on May 15, 1836, the ship anchored in Turon Bay, Cochin China.

Many modern Americans know this place intimately, but by another name. Americans — especially those who fought in the Vietnam War — know Da Nang, which Westerners once called Turon Bay, very well. The Pei-Ho River joins the sea here. (The television show *China Beach* took place in Da Nang.)

The land around the Turon Bay, or Da Nang, was sparsely populated at the time, but around 5 p.m. crew members were visited by three boats flying pennants, identifying them as representatives of the government. Roberts presented the officials who came aboard the *Peacock* with a letter written in French stating the purpose of the ship's visit. It was asked that these letters be delivered to Hue as quickly as possible because of the state of the ship's crew and Roberts himself, who was reported as being seriously indisposed.

The Cochin Chinese promised to reply within three days. On May 17, Cochin Chinese officials came out to the *Peacock*, and this time one of their party could speak Malay. There just happened to be a passenger on the *Peacock* who could speak Malay, so for the first time a constructive conversation could be had between both parties.

One of the problems that developed was that the Cochin Chinese did not believe Roberts was the envoy of the president of the United States, or even an important man. They dismissed him as being of little consequence, because he did not wear epaulettes or another insignia of rank like many of the officers aboard the ship; the Cochin Chinese reasoned that Roberts, therefore, could not be a significant personage.

This caused serious difficulty when the chief "mandarin" declared that it would be beneath his dignity to hold discussions with Mr. Roberts because he (the Cochin Chinese mandarin) had more titles and honors than Roberts and therefore outranked him significantly. Roberts disputed this and asked for a sheet of paper from the mandarin's secretary, who started to give him a half sheet.

Roberts refused this categorically and asked to be given a whole sheet of paper. When he received the piece of paper, he began by writing down his name, followed by the title "Esquire" (for gentleman), and then "Special Envoy from the President of the United States to the Emperor of Cochin China." He then began listing "Citizen of the United States," "Citizen of Maine," and "Citizen of New Hampshire," followed by all of the other states then part of the Union.

Before he was halfway through this ruse, the Cochin Chinese mandarin — who, of course, could not read English — was greatly impressed with this list as it grew, and grew, and grew. Somewhat flustered, the mandarin finally exclaimed that Roberts could stop, because he had already far exceeded the mandarin's "titles" and honorifics. If he had not been stopped, then it was Roberts plan to list every city, town, and village that he could remember — and perhaps invent a few.

On May 20, the mandarin sent fruit to the *Peacock* and informed Roberts that he would not have the answer to his letter for another eleven days. On May 21, the *Enterprise* finally caught up with the *Peacock* and arrived in Turon Bay. Like the ship it was supposedly escorting, the *Enterprise* had a very sick crew. On May 22, the mandarin returned to the *Peacock*, but Roberts was too sick to see him and the mandarin was sent away.

DEATH IN MACAO

From this point negotiations broke down. The Americans wanted to leave Turon Bay to get to a more salubrious harbor where the sick might have a better chance to recover. The *Peacock* and the *Enterprise* left Turon Bay the next day — May 23 — and sailed to Macao. They arrived on May 27, at which time the *Peacock* had five dead onboard. The cause of death was listed as dysentery.

In Macao, fresh provisions were brought onboard, but, meanwhile, thirty-two men and officers from the *Peacock* went to the hospital. More men were sent to the hospital on June 1, and on June 4, the captain of the *Enterprise* died. That same day, Roberts wrote to his children, relating that he was better and recovering from the diarrhea.

He outlined his plans for the future, saying that he could not return to Cochin China as planned because there were no interpreters. Since this mission was never completed and Roberts did not meet the Cochin Chinese emperor, it is assumed that the set of coins containing the 1804 Plain-4 Proof Eagle remained on the *Peacock* and was never delivered.

Roberts told his children that he planned to proceed to Japan and then to sail home from there by way of South America. This was highly optimistic, because on June 11, he became delirious. Roberts had evidently contracted dysentery in Siam, and some speculate that he also caught cholera. He died on June 12 in Macao while the *Peacock* was anchored in Cum-sing-moon harbor between Macao and Canton.

Some say Roberts passed away at the home of William S. Wetmore, reportedly the wealthiest American trader in Macao, but it is also mentioned that he died at the home of the British consul in Macao. In any event, it is known that he is buried in the Protestant cemetery in Macao.

On June 23, 1836, the *Peacock* and the *Enterprise* left Macao and sailed east toward home. Commodore Kennedy had originally been designated as Edmund Roberts's replacement should the latter become incapacitated, but Kennedy wrote to the State Department that the voyage to Japan was canceled, and that the diplomatic presents still onboard the *Peacock* — presumably including the two sets of coins intended for Japan and Cochin China — would be returned to the State Department by the first available vessel.

Exactly why Kennedy (the overall commander of the two-ship fleet) declined to finish Roberts's work is not known. It may be because he himself had become ill in Siam and wanted to bring home the crews of the two vessels before many more losses were sustained.

On July 2, 1836, the *Peacock* passed the island of Formosa and entered the Pacific Ocean. Although at least one more death from disease would occur a little later on, it was reported by the ship's surgeon that as soon as the ship left the China Sea and entered the Pacific, the various illnesses onboard began to abate.

Not until September 7, 1836, did the *Peacock* spot the Hawaiian island of Oahu, and on September 8 the ship anchored in Honolulu harbor, where it stayed for a month, until October 9. The *Peacock* sailed from Honolulu to Monterey, then the capital of upper California, which was part of Mexico. From there, the ship sailed southward along the California coast, down the length of Central and South America, and around Cape Horn to Rio de Janeiro. The *Peacock* finally arrived in Norfolk, Virginia, on October 27, 1837.

HALF DOLLAR
E PLURIBUS UNUM

CHAPTER ELEVEN

The 1804 Plain-4 Proof Eagles: Where Are They Now?

The U.S. State Department, after the end of the *Peacock*'s voyage and the return of the two undelivered sets of Proof coins, found itself in possession of two 1804 silver Dollars and two 1804 Plain-4 Proof Eagles. (The other 1804 silver Dollars were still at the Mint in Philadelphia.) These diplomatic presentation pieces were stored away in Washington, and there was no public announcement that these incredibly rare coins existed — and no collector suspected that such remarkable coins had ever been made.

THE 1804 SILVER DOLLAR

The fact that there were 1804 silver Dollars first came to light in 1842, when two Mint officials, W. E. DuBois and Jacob R. Eckfeldt, rather innocently published the book *A Manual of Gold and Silver Coins of All Nations, Struck within the Past Century* which, among other things, listed the contents of the U.S. Mint Cabinet. This cabinet was established in 1838, when chief coiner Adam Eckfeldt sold his private collection to the Mint to serve as a foundation for a collection of U.S. coins.

1785 Immune Columbia Coin in Gold (Photo courtesy of Professional Coin Grading Service, Inc.)

One of the illustrations was quite a surprise to many of the collectors of the day. It was of the 1804 silver Dollar, and it was not supposed to exist in any form or fashion. It was just identified as "Dollar, 1797–1805," but Matthew A. Stickney, a numismatist from Salem, Massachusetts, recognized it as a coin that was not known to hobbyists. That discovery must have sent an anticipatory thrill down Stickney's spine, and he became determined to acquire an example for his collection.

Stickney was interested in assembling a complete set of U.S. coins — and, of course, he did not have the 1804 silver Dollar, because it was not made for circulation that or any other year. He presented himself at the Mint on May 9, 1843, and began bargaining to acquire a specimen of the 1804 silver Dollar. He was prepared to trade rare coins for this piece, because at the time, the Mint valued the 1804 more than ordinary Proof coinage since it was not a regular production piece.

To obtain this piece, Stickney traded some Pine-Tree coins along with a rare "Immune Columbia" gold coin dated 1785, which is the only known example of this coin in gold. This rare piece can also be found in copper and silver. Most of these coins are dated 1785, but one type can be found dated 1787.

The Immune Columbia coins were pattern coins, somewhat similar to the "Nova Constellatio" silver and copper coins that first appeared dated 1783. These were not made for general circulation but were probably minted in a failed effort to secure a contract for copper coinage from the U.S. government under the Articles of Confederation.

While perusing the Mint Cabinet, Stickney noticed at least one other example of the 1804 silver Dollar, so he knew that his example was not unique, but all that was important to Stickney was that the coin filled a gap in his collection (a gap that should have never been filled), and he also understood the extreme rarity of the piece.

Over the next half-century, most of the original or "Class I" 1804 silver Dollars that had been minted during the period 1834–1835 entered private collections, some presumably through trades between numismatists and the Mint and others through circulation, where they were discovered soon after they left the Mint. Others were, of course, "liberated" from their cases at the State Department.

How these few specimens got into circulation is open to conjecture, but an inadvertent release is one possibility. Seven restrikes joined the "Class I" originals in the late 1850s, when Mint employees made these and other questionable copies of coins popular with collectors who had deep pockets. This was done in a small number of cases (including the 1804 Dollars) for personal gain, but most of the restrikes (e.g., the 1856 Flying Eagle Cents) were done under the authority of Mint Director James Ross Snowden, who used the new pieces to build up the Mint Cabinet through trade and other means.

THE 1804 PLAIN-4 PROOF EAGLES

We can trace the lives of these 1804 silver Dollars, but we are mainly concerned with the history of the much rarer 1804 Plain-4 Proof Eagle.

Knowledge of this coin was much slower to emerge than for the 1804 silver Dollar, and there is only sketchy documentation as to how these coins actually left the collection of the State Department or the set delivered to Oman.

The first public evidence of their existence was a photographic plate in *The American Journal of Numismatics* in 1869, which illustrated one without any special comment. Why this extremely rare coin with its colorful history did not cause instant hoopla is a bit of a mystery, but it might be because it looked very much like the much-less-rare 1804 Crosslet-4 Eagle — and the light just did not go on in the minds of numismatists. Collectors were of course well aware by 1869 that date varieties existed on the early coinage, and it was perhaps assumed that the Plain-4 coin was simply struck in 1804 from a variant obverse die.

It is agreed among experts that there are only four gold 1804 Plain-4 Proof Eagles in existence — but where are they now, and how did they get there? It is believed that the two sets of diplomatic gift coins that were never delivered to their intended recipients (the emperors of Japan and Cochin China) were returned to the United States, where they were broken up and sold in the same way the 1804 silver Dollar was to Mathew Stickney and others.

Unfortunately, no extant records exist regarding to whom these were sold, and for a very long time the 1804 Plain-4 Proof Eagles just vanished. No one seems to know how the two remaining 1804 Eagles left the State Department, but the first auction house sale of one occurred in March 1911 at the 48th Public Sale of well-known New York City coin dealer Thomas L. Elder.

The sale featured the collection of William H. Woodin, a prominent collector who served as secretary of the treasury under President Franklin Roosevelt some two decades later. As noted in the preface to his book, Elder got to sell a second specimen in 1935 when he sold the collections of E. H. Adams and F. Y. Parker, but there is no indication of how the coin was originally obtained.

Could these two coins sold by Elder be the two that were once destined for Japan and Cochin China, or were they once part of the Siamese or Omani sets? When the Omani government was queried about whether it still had its set, it did not express much interest in actually looking but said that the state coin collection was in bags stored on shelves behind one of the minister of state's desks, and that he was not inclined to go looking for it.

The Siamese set, however, is another matter altogether, because all but two of the coins from this set still reside in the original box. There is, however, some question as to whether or not the 1804 Plain-4 Eagle currently in the set is the original or a replacement. I frankly believe that it is a replacement, and that the real 1804 Eagle is the one I sold on two occasions. Let me explain. No one really knew of the existence of the "King of Siam" set until it surfaced in 1962 at the convention of the American Numismatic Association. Its history since being presented by Edmund Roberts to King Rama III (Nang Klao) in 1836 is a bit cloudy, but legend has it that it involves Anna Leonowens, the English teacher who was the subject of Margaret Landon's 1945 book *Anna and the King of Siam*.

A great deal of controversy surrounds this woman, and she seems to have "prettied up" her curriculum vitae just a bit. She claimed, for example, to have been born in 1834 in Wales, but modern research suggests that she was born in 1831 in India to an English cabinetmaker amd sergeant and a woman who was partly East Indian (at that time, a social stigma). Her maiden name appears to have been Ann Harriet Edwards.

Ann/Anna claimed to be the widow of an army officer, but in reality, she appears to have been wed to a civilian clerk (another step down the social ladder). For a time, she was indeed the English teacher to the children of Mongkut (King Rama V), but apparently she was not a "governess," as she later claimed in her writings. As the English teacher to the royal children, she succeeded Dan Beach Bradley.

When the coins were first sold in the late 1950s in London, the connection to the legendary King of Siam Proof set of coins surfaced when the sellers, who were two of Anna Leonowens's female descendants, claimed that the coins had come into Anna's possession and had been passed down in the family.

Some sources say the coins were a gift in appreciation of her services from King Rama IV, while other sources say she got them somewhat later from King Rama V (King Chulalongkom, who reigned from 1868 to 1910). A rather sly reference has been found that maintains Anna had a "liaison" with Chulalongkom, but who knows exactly what that might mean.

In any event, Leonowens left the employ of King Nang Klao shortly before his death and, reportedly, he did not press her to stay. She tried to return after his death in 1868, but the new King, Rama V, did not invite her. Anna and King Rama V (Chulalongkom), however, did meet again in London in 1897. Could the coin set have changed hands then? No one knows for sure. Leonowens died in 1915.

Since it surfaced to the public in 1962, the King of Siam Proof coin collection has been sold several times, with the last price being $8.5 million for the set. Currently, the set is in California, but there are several replacements in its current configuration, including a gold medalette featuring the image of President Andrew Jackson, the Half Dime, the Half Eagle, and the "King of Eagles" — the $10 1804 Plain-4 Proof Eagle.

How do I know? Well the dealer who sold the King of Siam set acknowledged to my father and me that the coin in his set was a replacement and, in fact, attempted three times to purchase the one we sold. In addition, I believe the coin we sold was originally from the King of Siam set, because when the pictures of the set as it was originally shown are compared to current pictures, it is evident to me that the coin currently in the King of Siam set is different and, therefore, a replacement.

In addition, my research reveals that a private collector wanted to buy the King of Eagles in 1961 and did in fact purchase it. There is absolutely no doubt in my mind that "our King of Eagles" is the one originally in the King of Siam set, because the finest specimens came from this collection. "Our" coin is a PF65 Ultra Cameo, and it is in the most pristine condition of all of the 1804 Plain-4 Proof Eagles made. This alone suggests that this is the coin Edmund Roberts delivered to the king of Siam.

I call this coin the "King of Eagles" because I believe it is the ultimate American coin in its beauty, rarity, and historic importance. In its beauty it is like a breathtaking painting executed by the ultimate master. Standing in front of it is a very moving experience, because it delivers such aesthetic impact and is indeed a work of art.

Its rarity cannot be questioned. Although it is generally agreed upon that four specimens of the 1804 Proof Eagle are known, for security reasons their present locations are not available — with one exception. That exception is the specimen owned by the Harry W. Bass Jr. Foundation, now on display at the museum of the American Numismatic Association in Colorado Springs. Another is in the privately held King of Siam set. The remaining two are in private collections, one of these being the King of Eagles that now belongs to one of my clients.

It is interesting to note that famed collector Louis Eliasberg actually owned two of these pieces at one time. In 1946, he sold the duplicate, and in October 1982, Bowers & Merena auctioned the other one; the latter coin is the specimen in the Bass collection.

Some people might argue that the 1933 Double Eagle is rarer, but this is not the case, as 445,525 of these coins were minted, but most were subsequently melted down. Two are in the Smithsonian, but a number left the Mint under unknown circumstances before they could be destroyed.

Several of these 1933 Double Eagles were discovered and confiscated by the federal government, but in 2002 one was allowed to be sold at auction (see the end of Chapter 5 for a more complete discussion of this event and the ramifications). It is my opinion that not all of the stolen 1933 Double Eagles have been recovered, and that there are at least one or two others in the hands of collectors, who are afraid to acknowledge their ownership because of the very real possibility of confiscation. (In 2005, as noted earlier, ten more pieces were turned over to the Mint for "authentication," and at present the matter is in the courts, as the Mint refuses to return them.)

As for the ultimate historical importance of the King of Eagles, it is beyond question. The 1804 Plain-4 Proof coin was the very first Proof Eagle ever made by the U.S. Mint, and that in itself is an important factor to numismatists. The four coins were ordered to be made by President Andrew Jackson as diplomatic gifts to heads of state in exotic lands, another fact that sets them apart from other American coins.

The King of Eagles was antedated, which is unprecedented in the history of the U.S. Mint. Technically, the coins were illegal when they were made, and they were made in a weight that was contrary to the laws in force in 1834. The four coins survived a long and harrowing sea voyage that involved an almost fatal shipwreck and pirate attack, and it is something of a miracle that they survived at all.

From a numismatic viewpoint, it is worth noting that there are 200 reeds on the edge of the King of Eagles, whereas the original gold Eagles of 1804 had only 126. It is merely one more difference that sets these special coins apart from those made in the early 1800s.

The history of the King of Eagles is one from which legends have been made, and it is perhaps the most romantic and historically important of all American coins. What, in my opinion, is the future of the 1804 Plain-4 Proof Eagle? Well, I believe it will be the first $10 million coin — and when that happens, the King of Eagles will take its rightful place at the very pinnacle of American coins.

APPENDIX

Treaty of Amity and Commerce between Siam and the United States

signed at Sia-Yut'hia (Bangkok), 20th March, 1833 [Ratifications exchanged at Bangkok, 14th April 1836]

His Majesty the Sovereign and Magnificent King in the City of Sia-Yut'hia, has appointed the Chau Phaya-Phraklang, one of the first Ministers of State, to treat with Edmund Roberts, Minister of the United States of America, who has been sent by the Government thereof, on its behalf, to form a treaty of sincere friendship and entire good faith between the two nations. For this purpose the Siamese and the citizens of the United States of America shall, with sincerity, hold commercial intercourse in the Ports of their respective nations as long as heaven and earth shall endure.

This Treaty is concluded on Wednesday, the last of the fourth month of the year 1194, called Pi-marong-chat-tavasok, or the year of the Dragon, corresponding to the 20th day of March, in the year of our Lord 1833. One original is written in Siamese, the other in English; but as the Siamese are ignorant of English, and the Americans of Siamese, a Portuguese and a Chinese translation are annexed, to serve as testimony to the contents of the Treaty. The writing is of the same tenor and date in all the languages aforesaid. It is signed on the one part, with the name of the Chau Phaya-Phraklang, and sealed with the seal of the lotus flower, of glass. On the other part, it is signed with the name of Edmund Roberts, and sealed with a seal containing an eagle and stars.

One copy will be kept in Siam, and another will be taken by Edmund Roberts to the United States. If the Government of the United States shall ratify the said Treaty, and attach the Seal of the Government, then Siam will also ratify it on its part, and attach the Seal of its Government.

ARTICLE I

There shall be a perpetual Peace between the Magnificent King of Siam and the United States of America.

ARTICLE II

The Citizens of the United States shall have free liberty to enter all the Ports of the Kingdom of Siam, with their cargoes, of whatever kind the said cargoes may consist; and they shall have liberty to sell the same to any of the subjects of the King, or others who may wish to purchase the same, or to barter the same for any produce or manufacture of the Kingdom, or other articles that may be found there. No prices shall be fixed by the officers of the King on the articles to be sold by the merchants of the United States, or the merchandise they may wish to buy, but the Trade shall be free on both sides to sell, or buy, or exchange, on the terms and for the prices the owners may think fit. Whenever the said citizens of the United States shall be ready to depart, they shall be at liberty so to do, and the proper officers shall furnish them with Passports: Provided always, there be no legal impediment to the contrary. Nothing contained in this Article shall be understood as granting permission to import and sell munitions of war to any person excepting to the King, who, if he does not require, will not be bound to purchase them; neither is permission granted to import opium, which is contraband; or to export rice, which cannot be embarked as an article of commerce. These only are prohibited.

ARTICLE III

Vessels of the United States entering any Port within His Majesty's dominions, and selling or purchasing cargoes of merchandise, shall pay in lieu of import and export duties, tonnage, license to trade, or any other charge whatever, a measurement duty only, as follows: The measurement shall be made from side to side, in the middle of the vessel's length; and, if a single-decked vessel, on such single deck; if otherwise, on the lower deck. On every vessel selling merchandise, the sum of 1700 Ticals, or Bats, shall be paid for every Siamese fathom in breadth, so measured, the said fathom being computed to contain 78 English or American inches, corresponding to 96 Siamese inches; but if the said vessel should come without merchandise, and purchase a cargo with specie only, she shall then pay the sum of 1,500 ticals, or bats, for each and every fathom before described. Furthermore, neither the aforesaid measurement duty, nor any other charge whatever, shall be paid by any vessel of the United States that enters a Siamese port for the purpose of refitting, or for refreshments, or to inquire the state of the market.

ARTICLE IV
If hereafter the Duties payable by foreign vessels be diminished in favour of any other nation, the same diminution shall be made in favour of the vessels of the United States.

ARTICLE V
If any vessel of the United States shall suffer shipwreck on any part of the Magnificent King's dominions, the persons escaping from the wreck shall be taken care of and hospitably entertained at the expense of the King, until they shall find an opportunity to be returned to their country; and the property saved from such wreck shall be carefully preserved and restored to its owners; and the United States will repay all expenses incurred by His Majesty on account of such wreck.

ARTICLE VI
If any citizen of the United States, coming to Siam for the purpose of trade, shall contract debts to any individual of Siam, or if any individual of Siam shall contract debts to any citizen of the United States, the debtor shall be obliged to bring forward and sell all his goods to pay his debts therewith. When the product of such bona fide sale shall not suffice, he shall no longer be liable for the remainder, nor shall the creditor be able to retain him as a slave, imprison, flog, or otherwise punish him, to compel the payment of any balance remaining due, but shall leave him at perfect liberty.

ARTICLE VII
Merchants of the United States coming to trade in the Kingdom of Siam and wishing to rent houses therein, shall rent the King's Factories, and pay the customary rent of the country. If the said merchants bring their goods on shore, the King's officers shall take account thereof, but shall not levy any duty thereupon.

ARTICLE VIII
If any citizens of the United States, or their vessels, or other property, shall be taken by pirates and brought within the dominions of the

Magnificent King, the persons shall be set at liberty, and the property restored to its owners.

ARTICLE IX

Merchants of the United States, trading in the Kingdom of Siam, shall respect and follow the laws and customs of the country in all points.

ARTICLE X

If thereafter any foreign nation other than the Portuguese shall request and obtain His Majesty's consent to the appointment of Consuls to reside in Siam, the United States shall be at liberty to appoint Consuls to reside in Siam, equally with such other foreign nation.

Whereas, the undersigned, Edmund Roberts, a citizen of Portsmouth, in the State of New Hampshire, in the United States of America, being duly appointed as Envoy, by Letters Patent, under the Signature of the President and Seal of the United States of America, bearing date at the City of Washington, the 26th day of January, in the year of our Lord 1832, for negotiating and concluding a Treaty of Amity and Commerce between the United States of America and His Majesty, the King of Siam.

Now know ye, that I, Edmund Roberts, Envoy as aforesaid, do conclude the foregoing Treaty of Amity and Commerce, and every Article and Clause therein contained; reserving the same, nevertheless, for the final Ratification of the President of the United States of America, by and with the advice and consent of the Senate of the said United States.

Done at the Royal City of Sia-Yut'hia (commonly called Bangkok), on the 20th day of March, in the year of our Lord 1833, and of the Independence of the United States of America the 57th.

EDMUND ROBERTS

Bibliography

Adams, Donald R. Jr. *Finance and Enterprise in Early America.* Philadelphia: University of Pennsylvania, 1978.

Akers, David W. *United States Gold Coins: An Analysis of Auction Records.* Volume 5 (Eagles, 1795–1933). Englewood, OH: Paramount, 1980.

Alexander, David T., Thomas K. DeLorey, and Brad Reed. *Coin World Comprehensive Catalog and Encyclopedia of United States Coins.* Sidney, OH: Amos Press, 1995.

The American Journal of Numismatics. New York: American Numismatic Society, August 1869.

The Annual Register or a View of History, Politics, and Literature. London, 1833–1836.

Attinelli, E. J. *Numisgraphics.* New York, 1876.

Bass, Harry W., Jr., and John W. Dannreuther. *Early U.S. Gold Coin Varieties.* Atlanta, GA: Whitman, 2006.

Benton, Thomas Hart. *Thirty Years' View or, A History of the Working of the American Government for Thirty Years, from 1820 to 1850.* 2 volumes. New York: D. Appleton and Company, 1854.

Blunt, Joseph. *The Shipmaster's Assistant and Commercial Digest.* New York: E. & G. W. Blunt, 1837.

Bowen, Charles. *The American Almanac and Repository of Useful Knowledge.* Boston, MA: Gray and Bowen, 1833–1836.

Bowers, Q. David. *American Numismatics before the Civil War.* Irvine, CA: Bowers & Merena, 1998.

———. *The Harry W. Bass Museum Sylloge.* Dallas, TX: Bass Foundation, 2001.

———. *The Rare Silver Dollars Dated 1804 and the Exciting Adventures of Edmund Roberts.* Irvine: CA: Bowers & Merena, 1999.

———. *Silver Dollars and Trade Dollars of the United States.* 2 volumes. Irvine, CA: Bowers & Merena, 1993.

Breen, Walter. *Walter Breen's Complete Encyclopedia of U.S. and Colonial Coins.* New York: Doubleday, 1988.

———. *Walter Breen's Encyclopedia of United States and Colonial Proof Coins, 1722–1977.* F.C.I. Press, 1977.

Callender, Guy S. *The Economic History of the United States, 1765–1860.* Kelley reprint, 1965.

Cobbett, William. *Life of Andrew Jackson.* London: 1834.

Comparette, T. L. *Catalogue of the Coins, Tokens, and Medals in the Numismatic Collection of the Mint of the United States at Philadelphia.* Washington, DC: Government Printing Office, 1912.

Cooper, Denis R. *The Art and Craft of Coinmaking.* London: Spink, 1988.

Crosby, Sylvester S. *Early Coins of America.* Boston, MA: 1875.

Davis, Charles. *American Numismatic Literature.* Lincoln, MA: Quarterman Publications, 1992.

Dickeson, Montroville W. *The American Numismatical Manual.* Philadelphia, PA: J. B. Lippincott & Co., 1859.

Dunbar, Charles F. *Laws of the United States Relating to Currency, Finance, and Banking.* Boston, MA: Ginn and Company, 1893.

Eckfeldt, Jacob R., and William E. Du Bois. *A Manual of Gold and Silver Coins of All Nations, Struck within the Past Century.* Philadelphia, PA: Mint Assay Office, 1842.

———. *New Varieties of Gold and Silver Coins.* New York: Putnam, 1851.

Elder, Thomas L. *Public Auction.* April 1935.

———. *Public Auction 48.* (Woodin collection) March 1911.

Evans, George. *Illustrated History of the United States Mint.* Philadelphia, PA: 1892.

Fielding, Mantle. *Dictionary of American Painters, Sculptors and Engravers.* Rev. ed. Modern Books, 1974.

Force, Peter. *The National Calendar and Annals of the United States, 1833–1836.* Washington, DC.

Frankel, Alison, "The Coin Chase." *The American Lawyer*, March 7, 2003.

———. *Double Eagle: The History of the $20 United States Gold Coin 1849–1933.* New York: Norton, 2006.

Frey, Albert R. *A Dictionary of Numismatic Names.* New York: American Numismatic Society, 1917.

Garrett, Jeff, and Ron Guth. *Encyclopedia of U.S. Gold Coins 1795–1933.* Atlanta, GA: Whitman, 2006.

Gerstell, Vivian S. *Silversmiths of Lancaster, Pennsylvania 1730–1850.* Lancaster, PA: Lancaster County Historical Society, 1972.

Gillilland, Cory. *Sylloge of the United States Holdings in the National Numismatic Collection of the Smithsonian Institution. Volume 1. Gold Coins, 1785–1834.* Washington, DC: Smithsonian Institution Press, 1992.

Grund, Francis J. *The Merchant's Assistant or Mercantile Instructor.* Boston, MA: 1834.

Haseltine, John. *Type Table of U.S. Dollars, Half Dollars & Quarter Dollars.* Philadelphia, PA: Bavis & Pennypacker, Steam Power Printers, 1881.

Hilt, Robert P. *Die Varieties of Early United States Coins.* Omaha, NE: RTS Publishing Co., 1980.

Jordan, Louis. *John Hull, The Mint, and the Economics of Massachusetts Coinage.* Lebanon, NH: University Press of New England, 2002.

Judd, J. Hewitt. *United States Pattern Coins, Experimental and Trial Pieces.* Atlanta, GA: Whitman, 2003.

Julian, R. W. *Medals of the United States Mint, The First Century 1792–1892.* Tokens and Medals Society, 1977.

———. "Origin of the 1804 Dollar." *The Numismatist*, January 1970.

Lanman, Charles. *Biographical Annals of the Civil Government of the United States.* J. M. Morrison, 1887.

Linderman, Henry R. *Money and Legal Tender.* Putnam, 1878.

Loewinger, Dr. Robert J. *Proof Gold Coinage of the United States.* Intrinsic Books, 2003.

Mayo, Dr. Robert. *Political Sketches of Eight Years in Washington.* Baltimore, MD: 1839.

Metcalf, William E., ed. *America's Gold Coinage.* New York: American Numismatic Society, 1990. ANS Symposium, November 1989.

Michels, Ivan. *The Current Gold and Silver Coins of All Nations.* Philadelphia, PA: R. S. Menamin, 1880.

Mint, U.S. Director of the. *Annual Reports*, 1795–1805 and 1834–1837.

Mossman, Philip L., ed. *Coinage of the American Confederation Period.* New York: American Numismatic Society, 1996. ANS Symposium, October 1995.

———. *Money of the American Colonies and Confederation.* New York: American Numismatic Society, 1993.

Newbold, T. J. *Political and Statistical Account of the British Settlements in the Straits of Malacca.* London: 1839.

Newman, Eric P. *Coinage for Colonial Virginia.* American Numismatic Society NNM 135, 1956.

———. *The Early Paper Money of America.* 4th edition. Iola, WI: Krause Publications, 1997.

———. "The James II 1/24th Real for the American Plantations." *Museum Notes XI*, American Numismatic Society, 1964.

———. "A Restated Opinion on the Origin of the 1804 Dollar and the 1804 Eagle Proofs." *America's Silver Dollars.* American Numismatic Society COAC 9, 1993.

———. *United States Fugio Copper Coinage of 1787.* Ypsilanti, MI: John Lusk, 2008.

Newman, Eric P., and Kenneth E. Bressett. *The Fantastic 1804 Dollar.* Atlanta, GA: Whitman, 1962.

Niles, H. *Niles' Weekly Register*, 1834–1836. Baltimore, MD.

Noe, Sydney P. *The Oak Tree Coinage of Massachusetts.* American Numismatic Society NNM 110, 1947.

———. *The Pine Tree Coinage of Massachusetts.* American Numismatic Society NNM 125, 1952.

Parton, James. *Life of Andrew Jackson.* 3 volumes. New York: Mason Brothers, 1860.

Pitkin, Timothy. *A Statistical View of the Commerce of the United States of America.* New Haven, CT: 1835.

Pollock, Andrew W. *United States Patterns and Related Issues.* Irvine, CA: Bowers & Merena, 1994.

Prime, W. C. *Coins, Medals, and Seals.* New York: Harper & Bothers Publishers, 1861.

Rantoul, Robert. *Eulogy on the Hon. Levi Woodbury*, October 16, 1851. Brewster, 1852.

Reed, P. Bradley, ed. *Coin World Almanac.* 6th edition. Jupiter, FL: Pharos Books, 1990.

Reiter, Ed. *The New York Times Guide to Coin Collecting.* New York: St. Martin's Press, 2002.

Reiver, Jules. *The United States Early Silver Dollars 1794 to 1803.* Iola, WI: Krause, 1999.

Representatives, U.S. House of. *Committee Report on Silver [and Gold].* 1831.

Riddell, J. L. *A Monograph of the Silver Dollar.* New Orleans, LA: 1845.

Roberts, Edmund. *Embassy to the Eastern Courts of Cochin China, Siam, and Muscat in the U.S. Sloop-of-War* Peacock, *David Geisinger, Commander, during the Years 1832–34.* Harper & Brothers Publishing, 1837.

Roberts, Edmund, and W. S. W. Ruschenberger. *Two Yankee Diplomats in 1830s Siam*, Itineraria Asiatica–Siam, Volume 10, edited by Michael Smither. Bangkok: Orchid Press, 2002.

Ruschenberger, W. S. W. *A Voyage Round the World, including an Embassy to Muscat and Siam.* Philadelphia, PA: 1838.

Schwartz, Ted. *A History of United States Coinage.* San Diego, CA, and New York: 1980.

Sellers, George E. "Early Engineering Reminiscences." *American Machinist*, (May–June 1893).

Smith, A. M. *Coins and Coinage.* Philadelphia, PA: 1881.

Snowden, James Ross. *A Description of Ancient and Modern Coins in the Cabinet Collection at the Mint of the United States.* Philadelphia, PA: J. B. Lippincott & Co., 1860.

Sotheby's. *Palace Collections of Egypt.* Auction sale brochure. 1954.

Stewart, Frank H. *History of the First United States Mint.* Reprinted edition. Lincoln, MA: Quarterman Publications, 1974.

Stickney, Matthew A. "More about the 1804 Silver Dollar." *American Journal of Numismatics*, August 1867.

Sumner, William G. *Andrew Jackson.* Boston, MA: Houghton, Mifflin and Company, 1898.

———. *A History of American Currency.* Originally published by Henry Holt & Co. in 1874. Reprinted edition. New York: Cosimo, Inc., 2005.

Taraszka, Anthony J. *United States Ten Dollar Gold Eagles, 1795–1804.* Portage, MI: Anton's, 1999.

Taxay, Donald P. *Scott's Comprehensive Catalogue and Encyclopedia of U.S. Coins 1971.* Scott, 1970.

———. *The U.S. Mint and Coinage.* New York: Arco, 1966.

The United States Gold Coin Collection. October 27–29. Irvine, CA: Bowers & Merena, 1982.

Van Ryzin, Robert R. *Twisted Tails.* Iola, WI: Krause, 1995.

Vermeule, Cornelius. *Numismatic Art in America.* Cambridge, MA: Harvard University Press, 1971.

Vlack, Robert A. *Early American Coins.* Johnson City, NY: Windsor Research Publications, 1965.

Weaver, William A. *Register of All Officers and Agents, Civil, Military, and Naval, in the Service of the United States on the Thirtieth of September 1835.* Washington, DC: 1835.

Williams, Edwin. *The New York Annual Register.* New York: 1833–1836.

Woodbury, Charles L. *Memoir of Hon. Levi Woodbury, LL.D.* 3 volumes. Boston, MA: 1894.

———. *Writings of Levi Woodbury, LL.D.* 3 volumes. New York: Little, Brown, 1852.

Yeoman, R. S. *A Guide Book of United States Coins 2008.* Atlanta, GA: Whitman, 2007.

Web Sites

www.coinlink.com
www.coinfact.com
www.wikipedia.com
www.oldcoinshop.com
www.law.com

Index

Photographs, paintings, and maps are indicated by *italic* page numbers.